Making Sense of
MAN
and
SIN

Works by Wayne Grudem

Bible Doctrine: Essential Teachings of the Christian Faith

Christian Beliefs: Twenty Basics Every Christian Should Know

Counterpoints: Are Miraculous Gifts for Today? (General Editor)

Politics According to the Bible

Systematic Theology

Systematic Theology Laminated Sheet

Making Sense of Series

Making Sense of the Bible

Making Sense of Who God Is

Making Sense of Man and Sin

Making Sense of Christ and the Spirit

Making Sense of Salvation

Making Sense of the Church

Making Sense of the Future

Making Sense of Man and Sin

One of Seven Parts from Grudem's
Systematic Theology

Wayne Grudem

ZONDERVAN

Making Sense of Man and Sin
Copyright © 1994, 2011 by Wayne Grudem

Previously published in *Systematic Theology*

This title is also available as a Zondervan ebook. Visit www.zondervan.com/ebooks.

Requests for information should be addressed to:

Zondervan, *Grand Rapids, Michigan* 49530

This edition: ISBN 978-0-310-49313-6 (softcover)

The Library of Congress has cataloged the complete volume as:

Grudem, Wayne Arden.
    Systematic theology: an introduction to biblical doctrine / Wayne Grudem.
       p.   cm.
    Includes index.
    ISBN 978-0-310-28670-7
    1. Theology, Doctrinal. I. Title.
BT75.2.G78 — 1994
230'.046—dc20   94-8300

Unless otherwise noted, Scripture quotations are taken from the *Revised Standard Version of the Bible*, copyright © 1946, 1952, 1971, by the Division of Christian Education of the National Council of Churches of Christ in the USA, and are used by permission. However, the author has, with permission, modernized archaic personal pronouns and has changed the verbs accordingly. Scripture quotations marked NASB are from the *New American Standard Bible*. Copyright © 1960, 1962, 1963, 1968, 1971, 1972, 1973, 1975, 1977, 1995 by the Lockman Foundation. Used by permission. Scripture quotations marked NIV are taken from the Holy Bible, *New International Version®, NIV®*. Copyright © 1973, 1978, 1984 by Biblica, Inc.™ Used by permission of Zondervan. All rights reserved worldwide. Use of italics in Scripture quotations indicates Wayne Grudem's emphasis.

Any Internet addresses (websites, blogs, etc.) and telephone numbers printed in this book are offered as a resource. They are not intended in any way to be or imply an endorsement by Zondervan, nor does Zondervan vouch for the content of these sites and numbers for the life of this book.

All rights reserved. No part of this publication may be reproduced, stored in a retrieval system, or transmitted in any form or by any means — electronic, mechanical, photocopy, recording, or any other — except for brief quotations in printed reviews, without the prior permission of the publisher.

Cover design: Rob Monacelli
Interior design: Mark Sheeres

Printed in the United States of America

CONTENTS

PREFACE   7

ABBREVIATIONS   11

   Chapter 1: Introduction to Systematic Theology   13

   Chapter 2: The Creation of Man   34

   Chapter 3: Man as Male and Female   48

   Chapter 4: The Essential Nature of Man   65

   Chapter 5: Sin   82

   Chapter 6: The Covenants Between God and Man   106

PREFACE

I have not written this book for other teachers of theology (though I hope many of them will read it). I have written it for students—and not only for students, but also for every Christian who has a hunger to know the central doctrines of the Bible in greater depth.

I have tried to make it understandable even for Christians who have never studied theology before. I have avoided using technical terms without first explaining them. And most of the chapters can be read on their own, so that someone can begin at any chapter and grasp it without having read the earlier material.

Introductory studies do not have to be shallow or simplistic. I am convinced that most Christians are able to understand the doctrinal teachings of the Bible in considerable depth, provided that they are presented clearly and without the use of highly technical language. Therefore I have not hesitated to treat theological disputes in some detail where it seemed necessary.

Yet this book is still an *introduction* to systematic theology. Entire books have been written about the topics covered in each chapter of this book, and entire articles have been written about many of the verses quoted in this book. Therefore each chapter is capable of opening out into additional study in more breadth or more depth for those who are interested. The bibliographies at the end of each chapter give some help in that direction.

The following six distinctive features of this book grow out of my convictions about what systematic theology is and how it should be taught:

1. A Clear Biblical Basis for Doctrines. Because I believe that theology should be explicitly based on the teachings of Scripture, in each chapter I have attempted to show where the Bible gives support for the doctrines under consideration. In fact, because I believe that the words of Scripture themselves have power and authority greater than any human words, I have not just given Bible references; I have frequently quoted Bible passages at length so that readers can easily examine for themselves the scriptural evidence and in that way be like the noble Bereans, who were "examining the scriptures daily to see if these things were so" (Acts 17:11). This conviction about the unique nature of the Bible as God's words has also led to the inclusion of a Scripture memory passage at the end of each chapter.

2. Clarity in the Explanation of Doctrines. I do not believe that God intended the study of theology to result in confusion and frustration. A student who comes out of a course in theology filled only with doctrinal uncertainty and a thousand unanswered questions is hardly "able to give instruction in sound doctrine and also to confute those who contradict it" (Titus 1:9). Therefore I have tried to state the doctrinal positions of this book clearly and to show where in Scripture I find convincing evidence for those positions. I do not expect that everyone reading this book will agree with me at every point of doctrine; I do think that every reader will understand the positions I am arguing for and where Scripture can be found to support those positions.

This does not mean that I ignore other views. Where there are doctrinal differences within evangelical Christianity I have tried to represent other positions fairly, to explain why I disagree with them, and to give references to the best available defenses of the opposing positions. In fact, I have made it easy for students to find a conservative evangelical statement on each topic from within their own theological traditions, because each chapter contains an index to treatments of that chapter's subject in thirty-four other theology texts classified by denominational background.

3. Application to Life. I do not believe that God intended the study of theology to be dry and boring. Theology is the study of God and all his works! Theology is meant to be lived and prayed and sung! All of the great doctrinal writings of the Bible (such as Paul's epistle to the Romans) are full of praise to God and personal application to life. For this reason I have incorporated notes on application from time to time in the text, and have added "Questions for Personal Application" at the end of each chapter, as well as a hymn related to the topic of the chapter. True theology is "teaching which accords with godliness" (1 Tim. 6:3), and theology when studied rightly will lead to growth in our Christian lives, and to worship.

4. Focus on the Evangelical World. I do not think that a true system of theology can be constructed from within what we may call the "liberal" theological tradition—that is, by people who deny the absolute truthfulness of the Bible, or who do not think the words of the Bible to be God's very words. For this reason, the other writers I interact with in this book are mostly within what is today called the larger "conservative evangelical" tradition—from the great Reformers John Calvin and Martin Luther, down to the writings of evangelical scholars today. I write as an evangelical and for evangelicals. This does not mean that those in the liberal tradition have nothing valuable to say; it simply means that differences with them almost always boil down to differences over the nature of the Bible and its authority. The amount of doctrinal agreement that can be reached by people with widely divergent bases of authority is quite limited. I am thankful for my evangelical friends who write extensive critiques of liberal theology, but I do not think that everyone is called to do that, or that an extensive analysis of liberal views is the most helpful way to build a positive system of theology based on the total truthfulness of the whole Bible. In fact, somewhat like the boy in Hans Christian Andersen's tale who shouted, "The Emperor has no clothes!" I think someone needs to say that it is doubtful that liberal theologians have given us any significant insights into the doctrinal teachings of Scripture that are not already to be found in evangelical writers.

It is not always appreciated that the world of conservative evangelical scholarship is so rich and diverse that it affords ample opportunity for exploration of different viewpoints and insights into Scripture. I think that ultimately we will attain much more depth of understanding of Scripture when we are able to study it in the company of a great number of scholars who all begin with the conviction that the Bible is completely true and absolutely authoritative. The cross-references to thirty-four other evangelical systematic theologies that I have put at the end of each chapter reflect this conviction: though they are broken down into seven broad theological traditions (Anglican/Episcopalian, Arminian/Wesleyan/Methodist, Baptist, Dispensational, Lutheran, Reformed/Presbyterian, and Renewal/Charismatic/ Pentecostal), they all would hold to the inerrancy of the Bible and would belong to what would be called a conservative evangelical position today. (In addition to these thirty-four conservative evangelical works, I have also added to each chapter a section of cross-references to two representative Roman Catholic theologies, because Roman Catholicism continues to exercise such a significant influence worldwide.)

5. Hope for Progress in Doctrinal Unity in the Church. I believe that there is still much hope for the church to attain deeper and purer doctrinal understanding, and to overcome old barriers, even those that have persisted for centuries. Jesus is at work perfecting his church "that he might present the church to himself in splendor, without spot or wrinkle or any such thing, that she might be holy and without blemish" (Eph. 5:27), and he has given gifts to equip the church "until we all attain to the unity of the faith and of the knowledge of the Son of God" (Eph. 4:13). Though the past history of the church may discourage us, these Scriptures remain true, and we should not abandon hope of greater agreement. In fact, in this century we have already seen much greater understanding and some greater doctrinal agreement between Covenant and Dispensational theologians, and between charismatics and noncharismatics; moreover, I think the church's understanding of biblical inerrancy and of spiritual gifts has also increased significantly in the last few decades. I believe that the current debate over appropriate roles for men and women in marriage and the church will eventually result in much greater understanding of the teaching of Scripture as well, painful though the controversy may be at the present time. Therefore, in this book I have not hesitated to raise again some of the old differences (over baptism, the Lord's Supper, church government, the millennium and the tribulation, and predestination, for example) in the hope that, in some cases at least, a fresh look at Scripture may provoke a new examination of these doctrines and may perhaps prompt some movement not just toward greater understanding and tolerance of other viewpoints, but even toward greater doctrinal consensus in the church.

6. A Sense of the Urgent Need for Greater Doctrinal Understanding in the Whole Church. I am convinced that there is an urgent need in the church today for much greater understanding of Christian doctrine, or systematic theology. Not only pastors and teachers need to understand theology in greater depth—the whole church does as well. One day by God's grace we may have churches full of Christians who can discuss, apply, and live the doctrinal teachings of the Bible as readily as they can discuss the details of their own jobs or hobbies—or the fortunes of their favorite sports team or television program. It is not that Christians lack the ability to understand doctrine; it is just that they must have access to it in an understandable form. Once that happens, I think that many Christians will find that understanding (and living) the doctrines of Scripture is one of their greatest joys.

"O give thanks to the LORD, for he is good; for his steadfast love endures for ever!"
(Ps. 118:29).

"Not to us, O Lord, not to us, but to your name give glory" (Ps. 115:1).

Wayne Grudem
Phoenix Seminary
4222 E. Thomas Road/Suite 400
Phoenix, Arizona 85018
USA

ABBREVIATIONS

BAGD	*A Greek-English Lexicon of the New Testament and Other Early Christian Literature.* Ed. Walter Bauer. Rev. and trans. Wm. Arndt, F. W. Gingrich, and F. Danker. Chicago: University of Chicago Press, 1979.
BDB	*A Hebrew and English Lexicon of the Old Testament.* F. Brown, S. R. Driver, and C. Briggs. Oxford: Clarendon Press, 1907; reprinted, with corrections, 1968.
BETS	*Bulletin of the Evangelical Theological Society*
BibSac	*Bibliotheca Sacra*
cf.	compare
CRSQ	*Creation Research Society Quarterly*
CT	*Christianity Today*
CThRev	*Criswell Theological Review*
DPCM	*Dictionary of Pentecostal and Charismatic Movements.* Stanley M. Burgess and Gary B. McGee, eds. Grand Rapids: Zondervan, 1988.
EBC	*Expositor's Bible Commentary.* Frank E. Gaebelein, ed. Grand Rapids: Zondervan, 1976.
ed.	edited by, edition
EDT	*Evangelical Dictionary of Theology.* Walter Elwell, ed. Grand Rapids: Baker, 1984.
et al.	and others
IBD	*The Illustrated Bible Dictionary.* Ed. J. D. Douglas, et al. 3 vols. Leicester: Inter-Varsity Press, and Wheaton: Tyndale House, 1980.
ISBE	*International Standard Bible Encyclopedia.* Revised edition. G. W. Bromiley, ed. Grand Rapids: Eerdmans, 1982.
JAMA	*Journal of the American Medical Association*
JBL	*Journal of Biblical Literature*
JETS	*Journal of the Evangelical Theological Society*
JSOT	*Journal for the Study of the Old Testament*
KJV	King James Version (Authorized Version)
LSJ	*A Greek-English Lexicon,* ninth edition. Henry Liddell, Robert Scott, H. S. Jones, R. McKenzie. Oxford: Clarendon Press, 1940.
LXX	Septuagint
mg.	margin or marginal notes
n.	note
n.d.	no date of publication given
n.p.	no place of publication given

NASB	New American Standard Bible
NDT	*New Dictionary of Theology.* S. B. Ferguson, D. F. Wright, J. I. Packer, eds. Leicester and Downers Grove, Ill.: InterVarsity Press, 1988.
NIDCC	*New International Dictionary of the Christian Church.* Ed. J. D. Douglas et al. Grand Rapids: Zondervan, 1974.
NIDNTT	*The New International Dictionary of New Testament Theology.* 3 vols. Colin Brown, gen. ed. Grand Rapids: Zondervan, 1975–78.
NIGTC	New International Greek Testament Commentaries
NIV	New International Version
NKJV	New King James Version
NTS	*New Testament Studies*
ODCC	*Oxford Dictionary of the Christian Church.* Ed. F. L. Cross. London and New York: Oxford University Press, 1977.
rev.	revised
RSV	Revised Standard Version
TB	*Tyndale Bulletin*
TDNT	*Theological Dictionary of the New Testament.* 10 vols. G. Kittel and G. Friedrich, eds.; trans. G. W. Bromiley. Grand Rapids: Eerdmans, 1964–76.
TNTC	Tyndale New Testament Commentaries
TOTC	Tyndale Old Testament Commentaries
trans.	translated by
TrinJ	*Trinity Journal*
vol.	volume
WBC	Word Biblical Commentary
WTJ	*Westminster Theological Journal*

Chapter 1

INTRODUCTION TO SYSTEMATIC THEOLOGY

What is systematic theology?
Why should Christians study it?
How should we study it?

EXPLANATION AND SCRIPTURAL BASIS

A. Definition of Systematic Theology

What is systematic theology? Many different definitions have been given, but for the purposes of this book the following definition will be used: *Systematic theology is any study that answers the question, "What does the whole Bible teach us today?" about any given topic.*[1]

This definition indicates that systematic theology involves collecting and understanding all the relevant passages in the Bible on various topics and then summarizing their teachings clearly so that we know what to believe about each topic.

1. Relationship to Other Disciplines. The emphasis of this book will not therefore be on *historical theology* (a historical study of how Christians in different periods have understood various theological topics) or *philosophical theology* (studying theological topics largely without use of the Bible, but using the tools and methods of philosophical reasoning and what can be known about God from observing the universe) or *apologetics* (providing a defense of the truthfulness of the Christian faith for the purpose of convincing unbe-

---

[1] This definition of systematic theology is taken from Professor John Frame, now of Westminster Seminary in Escondido, California, under whom I was privileged to study in 1971–73 (at Westminster Seminary, Philadelphia). Though it is impossible to acknowledge my indebtedness to him at every point, it is appropriate to express gratitude to him at this point, and to say that he has probably influenced my theological thinking more than anyone else, especially in the crucial areas of the nature of systematic theology and the doctrine of the Word of God. Many of his former students will recognize echoes of his teaching in the following pages, especially in those two areas.

lievers). These three subjects, which are worthwhile subjects for Christians to pursue, are sometimes also included in a broader definition of the term *systematic theology*. In fact, some consideration of historical, philosophical, and apologetic matters will be found at points throughout this book. This is because historical study informs us of the insights gained and the mistakes made by others previously in understanding Scripture; philosophical study helps us understand right and wrong thought forms common in our culture and others; and apologetic study helps us bring the teachings of Scripture to bear on the objections raised by unbelievers. But these areas of study are not the focus of this volume, which rather interacts directly with the biblical text in order to understand what the Bible itself says to us about various theological subjects.

If someone prefers to use the term *systematic theology* in the broader sense just mentioned instead of the narrow sense which has been defined above, it will not make much difference.[2] Those who use the narrower definition will agree that these other areas of study definitely contribute in a positive way to our understanding of systematic theology, and those who use the broader definition will certainly agree that historical theology, philosophical theology, and apologetics can be distinguished from the process of collecting and synthesizing all the relevant Scripture passages for various topics. Moreover, even though historical and philosophical studies do contribute to our understanding of theological questions, only Scripture has the final authority to define what we are to believe,[3] and it is therefore appropriate to spend some time focusing on the process of analyzing the teaching of Scripture itself.

Systematic theology, as we have defined it, also differs from *Old Testament theology, New Testament theology,* and *biblical theology.* These three disciplines organize their topics historically and in the order the topics are presented in the Bible. Therefore, in Old Testament theology, one might ask, "What does Deuteronomy teach about prayer?" or "What do the Psalms teach about prayer?" or "What does Isaiah teach about prayer?" or even, "What does the whole Old Testament teach about prayer and how is that teaching developed over the history of the Old Testament?" In New Testament theology one might ask, "What does John's gospel teach about prayer?" or "What does Paul teach about prayer?" or even "What does the New Testament teach about prayer and what is the historical development of that teaching as it progresses through the New Testament?"

"Biblical theology" has a technical meaning in theological studies. It is the larger category that contains both Old Testament theology and New Testament theology as we have defined them above. Biblical theology gives special attention to the teachings of *individual authors and sections* of Scripture, and to the place of each teaching in the *historical development* of Scripture.[4] So one might ask, "What is the historical development of the teaching about prayer as it is seen throughout the history of the Old Testament and then of the

---

[2]Gordon Lewis and Bruce Demarest have coined a new phrase, "integrative theology," to refer to systematic theology in this broader sense: see their excellent work, *Integrative Theology* (Grand Rapids: Zondervan, 1996). For each doctrine, they analyze historical alternatives and relevant biblical passages, give a coherent summary of the doctrine, answer philosophical objections, and give practical application.

[3]Charles Hodge says, "The Scriptures contain all the Facts of Theology" (section heading in *Systematic Theology,* 1:15). He argues that ideas gained from intuition or observation or experience are valid in theology only if they are supported by the teaching of Scripture.

[4]The term "biblical theology" might seem to be a natural and appropriate one for the process I have called

New Testament?" Of course, this question comes very close to the question, "What does the whole Bible teach us today about prayer?" (which would be *systematic theology* by our definition). It then becomes evident that the boundary lines between these various disciplines often overlap at the edges, and parts of one study blend into the next. Yet there is still a difference, for biblical theology traces the historical development of a doctrine and the way in which one's place at some point in that historical development affects one's understanding and application of that particular doctrine. Biblical theology also focuses on the understanding of each doctrine that the biblical authors and their original hearers or readers possessed.

Systematic theology, on the other hand, makes use of the material of biblical theology and often builds on the results of biblical theology. At some points, especially where great detail and care is needed in the development of a doctrine, systematic theology will even use a biblical-theological method, analyzing the development of each doctrine through the historical development of Scripture. But the focus of systematic theology remains different: its focus is on the collection and then the summary of the teaching of all the biblical passages on a particular subject. Thus systematic theology asks, for example, "What does the whole Bible teach us today about prayer?" It attempts to summarize the teaching of Scripture in a brief, understandable, and very carefully formulated statement.

2. Application to Life. Furthermore, systematic theology focuses on summarizing each doctrine as it should be understood by present-day Christians. This will sometimes involve the use of terms and even concepts that were not themselves used by any individual biblical author, but that are the proper result of combining the teachings of two or more biblical authors on a particular subject. The terms *Trinity, incarnation,* and *deity of Christ,* for example, are not found in the Bible, but they usefully summarize biblical concepts.

Defining systematic theology to include "what the whole Bible *teaches us* today" implies that application to life is a necessary part of the proper pursuit of systematic theology. Thus a doctrine under consideration is seen in terms of its practical value for living the Christian life. Nowhere in Scripture do we find doctrine studied for its own sake or in isolation from life. The biblical writers consistently apply their teaching to life. Therefore, any Christian reading this book should find his or her Christian life enriched and deepened during this study; indeed, if personal spiritual growth does not occur, then the book has not been written properly by the author or the material has not been rightly studied by the reader.

3. Systematic Theology and Disorganized Theology. If we use this definition of systematic theology, it will be seen that most Christians actually do systematic theology (or at least make systematic-theological statements) many times a week. For example: "The Bible says that everyone who believes in Jesus Christ will be saved." "The Bible says that Jesus Christ is the only way to God." "The Bible says that Jesus is coming again." These are all summaries of what Scripture says and, as such, they are systematic-

---

"systematic theology." However, its usage in theological studies to refer to tracing the historical development of doctrines throughout the Bible is too well established, so that starting now to use the term biblical theology to refer to what I have called systematic theology would only result in confusion.

theological statements. In fact, every time a Christian says something about what the whole Bible says, he or she is in a sense doing "systematic theology"—according to our definition—by thinking about various topics and answering the question, "What does the whole Bible teach us today?"[5]

How then does this book differ from the "systematic theology" that most Christians do? First, it treats biblical topics in a *carefully organized way* to guarantee that all important topics will receive thorough consideration. This organization also provides one sort of check against inaccurate analysis of individual topics, for it means that all other doctrines that are treated can be compared with each topic for consistency in methodology and absence of contradictions in the relationships between the doctrines. This also helps to ensure balanced consideration of complementary doctrines: Christ's deity and humanity are studied together, for example, as are God's sovereignty and man's responsibility, so that wrong conclusions will not be drawn from an imbalanced emphasis on only one aspect of the full biblical presentation.

In fact, the adjective *systematic* in systematic theology should be understood to mean something like "carefully organized by topics," with the understanding that the topics studied will be seen to fit together in a consistent way, and will include all the major doctrinal topics of the Bible. Thus "systematic" should be thought of as the opposite of "randomly arranged" or "disorganized." In systematic theology topics are treated in an orderly or "systematic" way.

A second difference between this book and the way most Christians do systematic theology is that it treats topics in *much more detail* than most Christians do. For example, an ordinary Christian as a result of regular reading of the Bible may make the theological statement, "The Bible says that everyone who believes in Jesus Christ will be saved." That is a perfectly true summary of a major biblical teaching. However, it can take several pages to elaborate more precisely what it means to "believe in Jesus Christ," and it could take several chapters to explain what it means to "be saved" in all of the many implications of that term.

Third, a formal study of systematic theology will make it possible to formulate summaries of biblical teachings with *much more accuracy* than Christians would normally arrive at without such a study. In systematic theology, summaries of biblical teachings must be worded precisely to guard against misunderstandings and to exclude false teachings.

Fourth, a good theological analysis must find and treat fairly *all the relevant Bible passages* for each particular topic, not just some or a few of the relevant passages. This often means that it must depend on the results of careful exegesis (or interpretation) of Scripture generally agreed upon by evangelical interpreters or, where there are significant differences of interpretation, systematic theology will include detailed exegesis at certain points.

---

[5]Robert L. Reymond, "The Justification of Theology with a Special Application to Contemporary Christology," in Nigel M. Cameron, ed., *The Challenge of Evangelical Theology: Essays in Approach and Method* (Edinburgh: Rutherford House, 1987), pp. 82–104, cites several examples from the New Testament of this kind of searching through all of Scripture to demonstrate doctrinal conclusions: Jesus in Luke 24:25–27 (and elsewhere); Apollos in Acts 18:28; the Jerusalem Council in Acts 15; and Paul in Acts 17:2–3; 20:27; and all of Romans. To this list could be added Heb. 1 (on Christ's divine Sonship), Heb. 11 (on the nature of true faith), and many other passages from the Epistles.

Because of the large number of topics covered in a study of systematic theology and because of the great detail with which these topics are analyzed, it is inevitable that someone studying a systematic theology text or taking a course in systematic theology for the first time will have many of his or her own personal beliefs challenged or modified, refined or enriched. It is of utmost importance therefore that each person beginning such a course firmly resolve in his or her own mind to abandon as false any idea which is found to be clearly contradicted by the teaching of Scripture. But it is also very important for each person to resolve not to believe any individual doctrine simply because this textbook or some other textbook or teacher says that it is true, unless this book or the instructor in a course can convince the student from the text of Scripture itself. It is Scripture alone, not "conservative evangelical tradition" or any other human authority, that must function as the normative authority for the definition of what we should believe.

4. What Are Doctrines? In this book, the word *doctrine* will be understood in the following way: *A doctrine is what the whole Bible teaches us today about some particular topic.* This definition is directly related to our earlier definition of systematic theology, since it shows that a "doctrine" is simply the result of the process of doing systematic theology with regard to one particular topic. Understood in this way, doctrines can be very broad or very narrow. We can speak of "the doctrine of God" as a major doctrinal category, including a summary of all that the Bible teaches us today about God. Such a doctrine would be exceptionally large. On the other hand, we may also speak more narrowly of the doctrine of God's eternity, or the doctrine of the Trinity, or the doctrine of God's justice.[6]

Within the major doctrinal category of this book, many more specific teachings have been selected as appropriate for inclusion. Generally these meet at least one of the following three criteria: (1) they are doctrines that are most emphasized in Scripture; (2) they are doctrines that have been most significant throughout the history of the church and have been important for all Christians at all times; (3) they are doctrines that have become important for Christians in the present situation in the history of the church (even though some of these doctrines may not have been of such great interest earlier in church history). Some examples of doctrines in the third category would be the doctrine of the inerrancy of Scripture, the doctrine of baptism in the Holy Spirit, the doctrine of Satan and demons with particular reference to spiritual warfare, the doctrine of spiritual gifts in the New Testament age, and the doctrine of the creation of man as male and female in relation to the understanding of roles appropriate to men and women today.

Finally, what is the difference between systematic theology and *Christian ethics?* Although there is inevitably some overlap between the study of theology and the study of ethics, I have tried to maintain a distinction in emphasis. The emphasis of systematic theology is on what God wants us to *believe* and to *know,* while the emphasis in Christian ethics is on what God wants us to *do* and what *attitudes* he wants us to have. Such a distinction is reflected in the following definition: *Christian ethics is any study that answers*

---

[6]The word *dogma* is an approximate synonym for *doctrine,* but I have not used it in this book. *Dogma* is a term more often used by Roman Catholic and Lutheran theologians, and the term frequently refers to doctrines that have official church endorsement. *Dogmatic theology* is another term for *systematic theology.*

the question, "What does God require us to do and what attitudes does he require us to have today?" with regard to any given situation. Thus theology focuses on ideas while ethics focuses on situations in life. Theology tells us how we should think while ethics tells us how we should live. A textbook on ethics, for example, would discuss topics such as marriage and divorce, lying and telling the truth, stealing and ownership of property, abortion, birth control, homosexuality, the role of civil government, discipline of children, capital punishment, war, care for the poor, racial discrimination, and so forth. Of course there is some overlap: theology must be applied to life (therefore it is often ethical to some degree). And ethics must be based on proper ideas of God and his world (therefore it is theological to some degree).

This book will emphasize systematic theology, though it will not hesitate to apply theology to life where such application comes readily. Still, for a thorough treatment of Christian ethics, another textbook similar to this in scope would be necessary.

B. Initial Assumptions of This Book

We begin with two assumptions or presuppositions: (1) that the Bible is true and that it is, in fact, our only absolute standard of truth; (2) that the God who is spoken of in the Bible exists, and that he is who the Bible says he is: the Creator of heaven and earth and all things in them. These two presuppositions, of course, are always open to later adjustment or modification or deeper confirmation, but at this point, these two assumptions form the point at which we begin.

C. Why Should Christians Study Theology?

Why should Christians study systematic theology? That is, why should we engage in the process of collecting and summarizing the teachings of many individual Bible passages on particular topics? Why is it not sufficient simply to continue reading the Bible regularly every day of our lives?

1. The Basic Reason. Many answers have been given to this question, but too often they leave the impression that systematic theology somehow can "improve" on the Bible by doing a better job of organizing its teachings or explaining them more clearly than the Bible itself has done. Thus we may begin implicitly to deny the clarity of Scripture or the sufficiency of Scripture.

However, Jesus commanded his disciples and now commands us also to *teach* believers to observe all that he commanded:

> Go therefore and make disciples of all nations, baptizing them in the name of the Father and of the Son and of the Holy Spirit, *teaching them* to observe all that I have commanded you; and lo, I am with you always, to the close of the age. (Matt. 28:19–20)

Now to teach all that Jesus commanded, in a narrow sense, is simply to teach the content of the oral teaching of Jesus as it is recorded in the gospel narratives. However, in a broader sense, "all that Jesus commanded" includes the interpretation and application of his life and teachings, because in the book of Acts it is implied that it contains a narrative of what Jesus *continued* to do and teach through the apostles after his resurrection (note that 1:1 speaks of "all that Jesus *began* to do and teach"). "All that Jesus commanded" can also include the Epistles, since they were written under the supervision of the Holy Spirit and were also considered to be a "command of the Lord" (1 Cor. 14:37; see also John 14:26; 16:13; 1 Thess. 4:15; 2 Peter 3:2; and Rev. 1:1–3). Thus in a larger sense, "all that Jesus commanded" includes all of the New Testament.

Furthermore, when we consider that the New Testament writings endorse the absolute confidence Jesus had in the authority and reliability of the Old Testament Scriptures as God's words, and when we realize that the New Testament epistles also endorse this view of the Old Testament as absolutely authoritative words of God, then it becomes evident that we cannot teach "all that Jesus commanded" without including all of the Old Testament (rightly understood in the various ways in which it applies to the new covenant age in the history of redemption) as well.

The task of fulfilling the Great Commission includes therefore not only evangelism but also *teaching*. And the task of teaching all that Jesus commanded us is, in a broad sense, the task of teaching what the whole Bible says to us today. To effectively teach ourselves and to teach others what the whole Bible says, it is necessary to *collect* and *summarize* all the Scripture passages on a particular subject.

For example, if someone asks me, "What does the Bible teach about Christ's return?" I could say, "Just keep reading your Bible and you'll find out." But if the questioner begins reading at Genesis 1:1 it will be a long time before he or she finds the answer to his question. By that time many other questions will have needed answers, and his list of unanswered questions will begin to grow very long indeed. What does the Bible teach about the work of the Holy Spirit? What does the Bible teach about prayer? What does the Bible teach about sin? There simply is not time in our lifetimes to read through the entire Bible looking for an answer for ourselves every time a doctrinal question arises. Therefore, for us to learn what the Bible says, it is very helpful to have the benefit of the work of others who have searched through Scripture and found answers to these various topics.

We can teach others most effectively if we can direct them to the most relevant passages and suggest an appropriate summary of the teachings of those passages. Then the person who questions us can inspect those passages quickly for himself or herself and learn much more rapidly what the teaching of the Bible is on a particular subject. Thus the necessity of systematic theology for teaching what the Bible says comes about primarily because we are finite in our memory and in the amount of time at our disposal.

The basic reason for studying systematic theology, then, is that it enables us to teach ourselves and others what the whole Bible says, thus fulfilling the second part of the Great Commission.

2. The Benefits to Our Lives. Although the basic reason for studying systematic theology is that it is a means of obedience to our Lord's command, there are some additional specific benefits that come from such study.

First, studying theology helps us *overcome our wrong ideas.* If there were no sin in our hearts, we could read the Bible from cover to cover and, although we would not immediately learn everything in the Bible, we would most likely learn only true things about God and his creation. Every time we read it we would learn more true things and we would not rebel or refuse to accept anything we found written there. But with sin in our hearts we retain some rebelliousness against God. At various points there are—for all of us—biblical teachings which for one reason or another we do not want to accept. The study of systematic theology is of help in overcoming those rebellious ideas.

For example, suppose there is someone who does not want to believe that Jesus is personally coming back to earth again. We could show this person one verse or perhaps two that speak of Jesus' return to earth, but the person might still find a way to evade the force of those verses or read a different meaning into them. But if we collect twenty-five or thirty verses that say that Jesus is coming back to earth personally and write them all out on paper, our friend who hesitated to believe in Christ's return is much more likely to be persuaded by the breadth and diversity of biblical evidence for this doctrine. Of course, we all have areas like that, areas where our understanding of the Bible's teaching is inadequate. In these areas, it is helpful for us to be confronted with the *total weight of the teaching of Scripture* on that subject, so that we will more readily be persuaded even against our initial wrongful inclinations.

Second, studying systematic theology helps us to be *able to make better decisions later on new questions of doctrine* that may arise. We cannot know what new doctrinal controversies will arise in the churches in which we will live and minister ten, twenty, or thirty years from now, if the Lord does not return before then. These new doctrinal controversies will sometimes include questions that no one has faced very carefully before. Christians will be asking, "What does the whole Bible say about this subject?" (The precise nature of biblical inerrancy and the appropriate understanding of biblical teaching on gifts of the Holy Spirit are two examples of questions that have arisen in our century with much more forcefulness than ever before in the history of the church.)

Whatever the new doctrinal controversies are in future years, those who have learned systematic theology well will be much better able to answer the new questions that arise. The reason for this is that everything that the Bible says is somehow related to everything else the Bible says (for it all fits together in a consistent way, at least within God's own understanding of reality, and in the nature of God and creation as they really are). Thus the new question will be related to much that has already been learned from Scripture. The more thoroughly that earlier material has been learned, the better able we will be to deal with those new questions.

This benefit extends even more broadly. We face problems of applying Scripture to life in many more contexts than formal doctrinal discussions. What does the Bible teach about husband-wife relationships? About raising children? About witnessing to a friend at work? What principles does Scripture give us for studying psychology, or economics, or the natural sciences? How does it guide us in spending money, or in saving, or in tithing? In every area of inquiry certain theological principles will come to bear, and those who have learned well the theological teachings of the Bible will be much better able to make decisions that are pleasing to God.

A helpful analogy at this point is that of a jigsaw puzzle. If the puzzle represents "what the whole Bible teaches us today about everything" then a course in systematic theology would be like filling in the border and some of the major items pictured in the puzzle. But we will never know everything that the Bible teaches about everything, so our jigsaw puzzle will have many gaps, many pieces that remain to be put in. Solving a new real-life problem is analogous to filling in another section of the jigsaw puzzle: the more pieces one has in place correctly to begin with, the easier it is to fit new pieces in, and the less apt one is to make mistakes. In this book the goal is to enable Christians to put into their "theological jigsaw puzzle" as many pieces with as much accuracy as possible, and to encourage Christians to go on putting in more and more correct pieces for the rest of their lives. The Christian doctrines studied here will act as guidelines to help in the filling in of all other areas, areas that pertain to all aspects of truth in all aspects of life.

Third, studying systematic theology will *help us grow as Christians.* The more we know about God, about his Word, about his relationships to the world and mankind, the better we will trust him, the more fully we will praise him, and the more readily we will obey him. Studying systematic theology rightly will make us more mature Christians. If it does not do this, we are not studying it in the way God intends.

In fact, the Bible often connects sound doctrine with maturity in Christian living: Paul speaks of "*the teaching which accords with godliness*" (1 Tim. 6:3) and says that his work as an apostle is "to further the faith of God's elect and their knowledge of *the truth which accords with godliness*" (Titus 1:1). By contrast, he indicates that all kinds of disobedience and immorality are "contrary to sound doctrine" (1 Tim. 1:10).

In connection with this idea it is appropriate to ask what the difference is between a "major doctrine" and a "minor doctrine." Christians often say they want to seek agreement in the church on major doctrines but also to allow for differences on minor doctrines. I have found the following guideline useful:

> A major doctrine is one that has a significant impact on our thinking about other doctrines, or that has a significant impact on how we live the Christian life. A minor doctrine is one that has very little impact on how we think about other doctrines, and very little impact on how we live the Christian life.

By this standard doctrines such as the authority of the Bible, the Trinity, the deity of Christ, justification by faith, and many others would rightly be considered major doctrines. People who disagree with the historic evangelical understanding of any of these doctrines will have wide areas of difference with evangelical Christians who affirm these doctrines. By contrast, it seems to me that differences over forms of church government or some details about the Lord's Supper or the timing of the great tribulation concern minor doctrines. Christians who differ over these things can agree on perhaps every other area of doctrine, can live Christian lives that differ in no important way, and can have genuine fellowship with one another.

Of course, we may find doctrines that fall somewhere between "major" and "minor" according to this standard. For example, Christians may differ over the degree of significance that should attach to the doctrine of baptism or the millennium or the extent of the atonement. That is only natural, because many doctrines have *some* influence on other doctrines or on life, but we may differ over whether we think it to be a "significant" influence. We could even recognize that there will be a range of significance here and just say that the more influence a doctrine has on other doctrines and on life, the more "major" it becomes. This amount of influence may even vary according to the historical circumstances and needs of the church at any given time. In such cases, Christians will need to ask God to give them mature wisdom and sound judgment as they try to determine to what extent a doctrine should be considered "major" in their particular circumstances.

D. A Note on Two Objections to the Study of Systematic Theology

1. "The Conclusions Are 'Too Neat' to be True." Some scholars look with suspicion at systematic theology when—or even because—its teachings fit together in a noncontradictory way. They object that the results are "too neat" and that systematic theologians must therefore be squeezing the Bible's teachings into an artificial mold, distorting the true meaning of Scripture to get an orderly set of beliefs.

To this objection two responses can be made: (1) We must first ask the people making the objection to tell us at what specific points Scripture has been misinterpreted, and then we must deal with the understanding of those passages. Perhaps mistakes have been made, and in that case there should be corrections.

Yet it is also possible that the objector will have no specific passages in mind, or no clearly erroneous interpretations to point to in the works of the most responsible evangelical theologians. Of course, incompetent exegesis can be found in the writings of the less competent scholars in *any* field of biblical studies, not just in systematic theology, but those "bad examples" constitute an objection not against the scholar's field but against the incompetent scholar himself.

It is very important that the objector be specific at this point because this objection is sometimes made by those who—perhaps unconsciously—have adopted from our culture a skeptical view of the possibility of finding universally true conclusions about anything, even about God from his Word. This kind of skepticism regarding theological truth is especially common in the modern university world where "systematic theology"—if it is studied at all—is studied only from the perspectives of philosophical theology and historical theology (including perhaps a historical study of the various ideas that were believed by the early Christians who wrote the New Testament, and by other Christians at that time and throughout church history). In this kind of intellectual climate the study of "systematic theology" as defined in this chapter would be considered impossible, because the Bible would be assumed to be merely the work of many human authors who wrote out of diverse cultures and experiences over the course of more than one thousand years: trying to find "what the whole Bible teaches" about any subject would be thought nearly as hopeless as trying to find "what all philosophers teach" about some question, for the answer in both cases would be thought to be not one view but many diverse and often conflicting views. This skeptical viewpoint must be rejected by evangelicals who see Scripture as the product of human *and* divine authorship, and therefore as a collection of writings that teach noncontradictory truths about God and about the universe he created.

(2) Second, it must be answered that in God's own mind, and in the nature of reality itself, *true* facts and ideas are all consistent with one another. Therefore if we have accurately understood the teachings of God in Scripture we should expect our conclusions to

"fit together" and be mutually consistent. Internal consistency, then, is an argument for, not against, any individual results of systematic theology.

2. "The Choice of Topics Dictates the Conclusions." Another general objection to systematic theology concerns the choice and arrangement of topics, and even the fact that such topically arranged study of Scripture, using categories sometimes different from those found in Scripture itself, is done at all. Why are *these* theological topics treated rather than just the topics emphasized by the biblical authors, and why are the topics *arranged in this way* rather than in some other way? Perhaps—this objection would say—our traditions and our cultures have determined the topics we treat and the arrangement of topics, so that the results of this systematic-theological study of Scripture, though acceptable in our own theological tradition, will in fact be untrue to Scripture itself.

A variant of this objection is the statement that our starting point often determines our conclusions on controversial topics: if we decide to start with an emphasis on the divine authorship of Scripture, for example, we will end up believing in biblical inerrancy, but if we start with an emphasis on the human authorship of Scripture, we will end up believing there are some errors in the Bible. Similarly, if we start with an emphasis on God's sovereignty, we will end up as Calvinists, but if we start with an emphasis on man's ability to make free choices, we will end up as Arminians, and so forth. This objection makes it sound as if the most important theological questions could probably be decided by flipping a coin to decide where to start, since *different* and *equally valid* conclusions will inevitably be reached from the different starting points.

Those who make such an objection often suggest that the best way to avoid this problem is not to study or teach systematic theology at all, but to limit our topical studies to the field of biblical theology, treating only the topics and themes the biblical authors themselves emphasize and describing the historical development of these biblical themes through the Bible.

In response to this objection, much of the discussion in this chapter about the necessity to teach Scripture will be relevant. Our choice of topics need not be restricted to the main concerns of the biblical authors, for our goal is to find out what God requires of us in all areas of concern to us today.

For example, it was not the *main* concern of any New Testament author to explain such topics as "baptism in the Holy Spirit," or women's roles in the church, or the doctrine of the Trinity, but these are valid areas of concern for us today, and we must look at all the places in Scripture that have relevance for those topics (whether those specific terms are mentioned or not, and whether those themes are of primary concern to each passage we examine or not) if we are going to be able to understand and explain to others "what the whole Bible teaches" about them.

The only alternative—for we *will* think *something* about those subjects—is to form our opinions haphazardly from a general impression of what we feel to be a "biblical" position on each subject, or perhaps to buttress our positions with careful analysis of one or two relevant texts, yet with no guarantee that those texts present a balanced view of "the whole counsel of God" (Acts 20:27) on the subject being considered. In fact this approach—one all too common in evangelical circles today—could, I suppose, be called "unsystematic theology" or even "disorderly and random theology"! Such an alternative is too subjective and too subject to cultural pressures. It tends toward doctrinal fragmentation and widespread doctrinal uncertainty, leaving the church theologically immature, like "children, tossed to and fro and carried about with every wind of doctrine" (Eph. 4:14).

Concerning the objection about the choice and sequence of topics, there is nothing to prevent us from going to Scripture to look for answers to *any* doctrinal questions, considered in *any sequence.* The sequence of topics in this book is a very common one and has been adopted because it is orderly and lends itself well to learning and teaching. But the chapters could be read in any sequence one wanted and the conclusions should not be different, nor should the persuasiveness of the arguments—if they are rightly derived from Scripture—be significantly diminished. I have tried to write the chapters so that they can be read as independent units.

E. How Should Christians Study Systematic Theology?

How then should we study systematic theology? The Bible provides some guidelines for answering this question.

1. We Should Study Systematic Theology With Prayer. If studying systematic theology is simply a certain way of studying the Bible, then the passages in Scripture that talk about the way in which we should study God's Word give guidance to us in this task. Just as the psalmist prays in Psalm 119:18, "Open my eyes, that I may behold wondrous things out of your law," so we should pray and seek God's help in understanding his Word. Paul tells us in 1 Corinthians 2:14 that "the unspiritual man does not receive the gifts of the Spirit of God, for they are folly to him, and he is not able to understand them because they are spiritually discerned." Studying theology is therefore a spiritual activity in which we need the help of the Holy Spirit.

No matter how intelligent, if the student does not continue to pray for God to give him or her an understanding mind and a believing and humble heart, and the student does not maintain a personal walk with the Lord, then the teachings of Scripture will be misunderstood and disbelieved, doctrinal error will result, and the mind and heart of the student will not be changed for the better but for the worse. Students of systematic theology should resolve at the beginning to keep their lives free from any disobedience to God or any known sin that would disrupt their relationship with him. They should resolve to maintain with great regularity their own personal devotional lives. They should continually pray for wisdom and understanding of Scripture.

Since it is the Holy Spirit who gives us the ability rightly to understand Scripture, we need to realize that the proper thing to do, particularly when we are unable to understand some passage or some doctrine of Scripture, is to pray for God's help. Often what we need is not more data but more insight into the data we already have available. This insight is given only by the Holy Spirit (cf. 1 Cor. 2:14; Eph. 1:17–19).

2. We Should Study Systematic Theology With Humility. Peter tells us, "Clothe yourselves, all of you, with humility toward one another, for 'God opposes the proud, but gives grace to the humble'" (1 Peter 5:5). Those who study systematic theology will learn many things about the teachings of Scripture that are perhaps not known or not known well by other Christians in their churches or by relatives who are older in the Lord than they are. They may also find that they understand things about Scripture that some of their church officers do not understand, and that even their pastor has perhaps forgotten or never learned well.

In all of these situations it would be very easy to adopt an attitude of pride or superiority toward others who have not made such a study. But how ugly it would be if anyone were to use this knowledge of God's Word simply to win arguments or to put down a fellow Christian in conversation, or to make another believer feel insignificant in the Lord's work. James' counsel is good for us at this point: "Let every man be quick to hear, slow to speak, slow to anger, for the anger of man does not work the righteousness of God" (James 1:19–20). He tells us that one's understanding of Scripture is to be imparted in humility and love:

> Who is wise and understanding among you? By his good life let him show his works in the meekness of wisdom.... But the wisdom from above is first pure, then peaceable, gentle, open to reason, full of mercy and good fruits, without uncertainty or insincerity. And the harvest of righteousness is sown in peace by those who make peace. (James 3:13, 17–18)

Systematic theology rightly studied will not lead to the knowledge that "puffs up" (1 Cor. 8:1) but to humility and love for others.

3. We Should Study Systematic Theology With Reason. We find in the New Testament that Jesus and the New Testament authors will often quote a verse of Scripture and then draw logical conclusions from it. They *reason* from Scripture. It is therefore not wrong to use human understanding, human logic, and human reason to draw conclusions from the statements of Scripture. Nevertheless, when we reason and draw what we think to be correct logical deductions from Scripture, we sometimes make mistakes. The deductions we draw from the statements of Scripture are not equal to the statements of Scripture themselves in certainty or authority, for our ability to reason and draw conclusions is not the ultimate standard of truth—only Scripture is.

What then are the limits on our use of our reasoning abilities to draw deductions from the statements of Scripture? The fact that reasoning to conclusions that go beyond the mere statements of Scripture is appropriate and even necessary for studying Scripture, and the fact that Scripture itself is the ultimate standard of truth, combine to indicate to us that *we are free to use our reasoning abilities to draw deductions from any passage of Scripture so long as these deductions do not contradict the clear teaching of some other passage of Scripture.*[7]

This principle puts a safeguard on our use of what we think to be logical deductions from Scripture. Our supposedly logical deductions may be erroneous, but Scripture itself cannot be erroneous. Thus, for example, we may read Scripture and find that God the Father is called God (1 Cor. 1:3), that God the Son is called God (John 20:28; Titus 2:13), and that God the Holy Spirit is called God (Acts 5:3–4). We might deduce from this that there are three Gods. But then we find the Bible explicitly teaching us that God is one

(Deut. 6:4; James 2:19). Thus we conclude that what we *thought* to be a valid logical deduction about three Gods was wrong and that Scripture teaches both (a) that there are three separate persons (the Father, the Son, and the Holy Spirit), each of whom is fully God, and (b) that there is one God.

We cannot understand exactly how these two statements can both be true, so together they constitute a *paradox* ("a seemingly contradictory statement that may nonetheless be true").[8] We can tolerate a paradox (such as "God is three persons and one God") because we have confidence that ultimately God knows fully the truth about himself and about the nature of reality, and that in his understanding the different elements of a paradox are fully reconciled, even though at this point God's thoughts are higher than our thoughts (Isa. 55:8–9). But a true contradiction (such as, "God is three persons and God is not three persons") would imply ultimate contradiction in God's own understanding of himself or of reality, and this cannot be.

When the psalmist says, "The sum of your word is truth; and every one of your righteous ordinances endures for ever" (Ps. 119:160), he implies that God's words are not only true individually but also viewed together as a whole. Viewed collectively, their "sum" is also "truth." Ultimately, there is no internal contradiction either in Scripture or in God's own thoughts.

4. We Should Study Systematic Theology With Help From Others. We need to be thankful that God has put teachers in the church ("And God has appointed in the church

---

[7]This guideline is also adopted from Professor John Frame at Westminster Seminary.

[8]The *American Heritage Dictionary of the English Language*, ed. William Morris (Boston: Houghton-Mifflin, 1980), p. 950 (first definition). Essentially the same meaning is adopted by the *Oxford English Dictionary* (1913 ed., 7:450), the *Concise Oxford Dictionary* (1981 ed., p. 742), the *Random House College Dictionary* (1979 ed., p. 964), and the *Chambers Twentieth Century Dictionary* (p. 780), though all note that *paradox* can also mean "contradiction" (though less commonly); compare the *Encyclopedia of Philosophy*, ed. Paul Edwards (New York: Macmillan and The Free Press, 1967), 5:45, and the entire article "Logical Paradoxes" by John van Heijenoort on pp. 45–51 of the same volume, which proposes solutions to many of the classical paradoxes in the history of philosophy. (If *paradox* meant "contradiction," such solutions would be impossible.)

When I use the word *paradox* in the primary sense defined by these dictionaries today I realize that I am differing somewhat with the article "Paradox" by K. S. Kantzer in the *EDT*, ed. Walter Elwell, pp. 826–27 (which takes *paradox* to mean essentially "contradiction"). However, I am using *paradox* in an ordinary English sense and one also familiar in philosophy. There seems to me to be available no better word than *paradox* to refer to an apparent but not real contradiction.

There is, however, some lack of uniformity in the use of the term *paradox* and a related term, *antinomy,* in contemporary evangelical discussion. The word *antinomy* has sometimes been used to apply to what I here call *paradox,* that is, "seemingly contradictory statements that may nonetheless both be true" (see, for example, John Jefferson Davis, *Theology Primer* [Grand Rapids: Baker, 1981], p. 18). Such a sense for *antinomy* gained support in a widely read book, *Evangelism and the Sovereignty of God,* by J. I. Packer (London: Inter-Varsity Press, 1961). On pp. 18–22 Packer defines *antinomy* as "an appearance of contradiction" (but admits on p. 18 that his definition differs with the *Shorter Oxford Dictionary*). My problem with using *antinomy* in this sense is that the word is so unfamiliar in ordinary English that it just increases the stock of technical terms Christians have to learn in order to understand theologians, and moreover such a sense is unsupported by any of the dictionaries cited above, all of which define *antinomy* to mean "contradiction" (e.g., *Oxford English Dictionary,* 1:371). The problem is not serious, but it would help communication if evangelicals could agree on uniform senses for these terms.

A paradox is certainly acceptable in systematic theology, and paradoxes are in fact inevitable so long as we have finite understanding of any theological topic. However, it is important to recognize that Christian theology should never affirm a *contradiction* (a set of two statements, one of which denies the other). A contradiction would be, "God is three persons and God is not three persons" (where the term *persons* has the same sense in both halves of the sentence).

first apostles, second prophets, third *teachers* . . ." [1 Cor. 12:28]. We should allow those with gifts of teaching to help us understand Scripture. This means that we should make use of systematic theologies and other books that have been written by some of the teachers that God has given to the church over the course of its history. It also means that our study of theology should include *talking with other Christians* about the things we study. Among those with whom we talk will often be some with gifts of teaching who can explain biblical teachings clearly and help us to understand more easily. In fact, some of the most effective learning in systematic theology courses in colleges and seminaries often occurs outside the classroom in informal conversations among students who are attempting to understand Bible doctrines for themselves.

5. We Should Study Systematic Theology by Collecting and Understanding All the Relevant Passages of Scripture on Any Topic. This point was mentioned in our definition of systematic theology at the beginning of the chapter, but the actual process needs to be described here. How does one go about making a doctrinal summary of what all the passages of Scripture teach on a certain topic? For topics covered in this book, many people will think that studying the chapters in this book and reading the Bible verses noted in the chapters is enough. But some people will want to do further study of Scripture on a particular topic or study some new topic not covered here. How could a student go about using the Bible to research its teachings on some new subject, perhaps one not discussed explicitly in any of his or her systematic theology textbooks?

The process would look like this: (1) Find all the relevant verses. The best help in this step is a good concordance, which enables one to look up key words and find the verses in which the subject is treated. For example, in studying what it means that man is created in the image and likeness of God, one needs to find all the verses in which "image" and "likeness" and "create" occur. (The words "man" and "God" occur too often to be useful for a concordance search.) In studying the doctrine of prayer, many words could be looked up (*pray, prayer, intercede, petition, supplication, confess, confession, praise, thanks, thanksgiving,* et al.) — and perhaps the list of verses would grow too long to be manageable, so that the student would have to skim the concordance entries without looking up the verses, or the search would probably have to be divided into sections or limited in some other way. Verses can also be found by thinking through the overall history of the Bible and then turning to sections where there would be information on the topic at hand — for example, a student studying prayer would want to read passages like the one about Hannah's prayer for a son (in 1 Sam. 1), Solomon's prayer at the dedication of the temple (in 1 Kings 8), Jesus' prayer in the Garden of Gethsemane (in Matt. 26 and parallels), and so forth. Then in addition to concordance work and reading other passages that one can find on the subject, checking the relevant sections in some systematic theology books will often bring to light other verses that had been missed, sometimes because none of the key words used for the concordance were in those verses.[9]

(2) The second step is to read, make notes on, and try to summarize the points made in the relevant verses. Sometimes a theme will be repeated often and the summary of the various verses will be relatively easy. At other times, there will be verses difficult to understand, and the student will need to take some time to study a verse in depth

(just by reading the verse in context over and over, or by using specialized tools such as commentaries and dictionaries) until a satisfactory understanding is reached.

(3) Finally, the teachings of the various verses should be summarized into one or more points that the Bible affirms about that subject. The summary does not have to take the exact form of anyone else's conclusions on the subject, because we each may see things in Scripture that others have missed, or we may organize the subject differently or emphasize different things.

On the other hand, at this point it is also helpful to read related sections, if any can be found, in several systematic theology books. This provides a useful check against error and oversight, and often makes one aware of alternative perspectives and arguments that may cause us to modify or strengthen our position. If a student finds that others have argued for strongly differing conclusions, then these other views need to be stated fairly and then answered. Sometimes other theology books will alert us to historical or philosophical considerations that have been raised before in the history of the church, and these will provide additional insight or warnings against error.

The process outlined above is possible for any Christian who can read his or her Bible and can look up words in a concordance. Of course people will become faster and more accurate in this process with time and experience and Christian maturity, but it would be a tremendous help to the church if Christians generally would give much more time to searching out topics in Scripture for themselves and drawing conclusions in the way outlined above. The joy of discovery of biblical themes would be richly rewarding. Especially pastors and those who lead Bible studies would find added freshness in their understanding of Scripture and in their teaching.

6. We Should Study Systematic Theology With Rejoicing and Praise. The study of theology is not merely a theoretical exercise of the intellect. It is a study of the living God, and of the wonders of all his works in creation and redemption. We cannot study this subject dispassionately! We must love all that God is, all that he says and all that he does. "You shall love the LORD your God with all your heart" (Deut. 6:5). Our response to the study of the theology of Scripture should be that of the psalmist who said, "How precious to me are your thoughts, O God!" (Ps. 139:17). In the study of the teachings of God's Word, it should not surprise us if we often find our hearts spontaneously breaking forth in expressions of praise and delight like those of the psalmist:

> The precepts of the LORD are right,
>   rejoicing the heart. (Ps. 19:8)

> In the way of your testimonies I delight
>   as much as in all riches. (Ps. 119:14)

> How sweet are your words to my taste,

---

[9] I have read a number of student papers telling me that John's gospel says nothing about how Christians should pray, for example, because they looked at a concordance and found that the word *prayer* was not in John, and the word *pray* only occurs four times in reference to Jesus praying in John 14, 16, and 17. They overlooked the fact that John contains several important verses where the word *ask* rather than the word *pray* is used (John 14:13–14; 15:7, 16, et al.).

> sweeter than honey to my mouth! (Ps. 119:103)

> Your testimonies are my heritage for ever;
> yea, they are the joy of my heart. (Ps. 119:111)

> I rejoice at your word
> like one who finds great spoil. (Ps. 119:162)

Often in the study of theology the response of the Christian should be similar to that of Paul in reflecting on the long theological argument that he has just completed at the end of Romans 11:32. He breaks forth into joyful praise at the richness of the doctrine which God has enabled him to express:

> O the depth of the riches and wisdom and knowledge of God! How unsearchable are his judgments and how inscrutable his ways!

> "For who has known the mind of the Lord,
> or who has been his counselor?"
> "Or who has given a gift to him
> that he might be repaid?"

> For from him and through him and to him are all things. To him be glory for ever. Amen. (Rom. 11:33–36)

QUESTIONS FOR PERSONAL APPLICATION

These questions at the end of each chapter focus on application to life. Because I think doctrine is to be felt at the emotional level as well as understood at the intellectual level, in many chapters I have included some questions about how a reader *feels* regarding a point of doctrine. I think these questions will prove quite valuable for those who take the time to reflect on them.

1. In what ways (if any) has this chapter changed your understanding of what systematic theology is? What was your attitude toward the study of systematic theology before reading this chapter? What is your attitude now?

2. What is likely to happen to a church or denomination that gives up learning systematic theology for a generation or longer? Has that been true of your church?

3. Are there any doctrines listed in the Contents for which a fuller understanding would help to solve a personal difficulty in your life at the present time? What are the spiritual and emotional dangers that you personally need to be aware of in studying systematic theology?

4. Pray for God to make this study of basic Christian doctrines a time of spiritual growth and deeper fellowship with him, and a time in which you understand and apply the teachings of Scripture rightly.

SPECIAL TERMS

apologetics
biblical theology
Christian ethics
contradiction
doctrine
dogmatic theology
historical theology
major doctrine

minor doctrine
New Testament theology
Old Testament theology
paradox
philosophical theology
presupposition
systematic theology

BIBLIOGRAPHY

Baker, D. L. "Biblical Theology." In *NDT*, p. 671.

Berkhof, Louis. *Introduction to Systematic Theology*. Grand Rapids: Eerdmans, 1982, pp. 15–75 (first published 1932).

Bray, Gerald L., ed. *Contours of Christian Theology*. Downers Grove, Ill.: InterVarsity Press, 1993.

_____. "Systematic Theology, History of." In *NDT*, pp. 671–72.

Cameron, Nigel M., ed. *The Challenge of Evangelical Theology: Essays in Approach and Method*. Edinburgh: Rutherford House, 1987.

Carson, D. A. "Unity and Diversity in the New Testament: The Possibility of Systematic Theology." In *Scripture and Truth*. Ed. by D. A. Carson and John Woodbridge. Grand Rapids: Zondervan, 1983, pp. 65–95.

Davis, John Jefferson. *Foundations of Evangelical Theology*. Grand Rapids: Baker, 1984.

_____. *The Necessity of Systematic Theology*. Grand Rapids: Baker, 1980.

_____. *Theology Primer: Resources for the Theological Student*. Grand Rapids: Baker, 1981.

Demarest, Bruce. "Systematic Theology." In *EDT*, pp. 1064–66.

Erickson, Millard. *Concise Dictionary of Christian Theology*. Grand Rapids: Baker, 1986.

Frame, John. *Van Til the Theologian*. Phillipsburg, N.J.: Pilgrim, 1976.

Geehan, E. R., ed. *Jerusalem and Athens*. Nutley, N.J.: Craig Press, 1971.

Grenz, Stanley J. *Revisioning Evangelical Theology: A Fresh Agenda for the 21st Century*. Downers Grove, Ill.: InterVarsity Press, 1993.

House, H. Wayne. *Charts of Christian Theology and Doctrine*. Grand Rapids: Zondervan, 1992.

Kuyper, Abraham. *Principles of Sacred Theology*. Trans. by J. H. DeVries. Grand Rapids: Eerdmans, 1968 (reprint; first published as *Encyclopedia of Sacred Theology* in 1898).

Machen, J. Gresham. *Christianity and Liberalism*. Grand Rapids: Eerdmans, 1923. (This 180-page book is, in my opinion, one of the most significant theological studies ever written. It gives a clear overview of major biblical doctrines and shows the vital differences with Protestant liberal theology at every point, differences that still confront us today. It is required reading in all my introductory theology classes.)

Morrow, T. W. "Systematic Theology." In *NDT*, p. 671.

Poythress, Vern. *Symphonic Theology: The Validity of Multiple Perspectives in Theology.* Grand Rapids: Zondervan, 1987.

Preus, Robert D. *The Theology of Post-Reformation Lutheranism: A Study of Theological Prolegomena.* 2 vols. St. Louis: Concordia, 1970.

Van Til, Cornelius. *In Defense of the Faith*, vol. 5: *An Introduction to Systematic Theology.* N.p.: Presbyterian and Reformed, 1976, pp. 1–61, 253–62.

_____. *The Defense of the Faith.* Philadelphia: Presbyterian and Reformed, 1955.

Vos, Geerhardus. "The Idea of Biblical Theology as a Science and as a Theological Discipline." In *Redemptive History and Biblical Interpretation,* pp. 3–24. Ed. by Richard Gaffin. Phillipsburg, N.J.: Presbyterian and Reformed, 1980 (article first published 1894).

Warfield, B. B. "The Indispensableness of Systematic Theology to the Preacher." In *Selected Shorter Writings of Benjamin B. Warfield,* 2:280–88. Ed. by John E. Meeter. Nutley, N.J.: Presbyterian and Reformed, 1973 (article first published 1897).

_____. "The Right of Systematic Theology." In *Selected Shorter Writings of Benjamin B. Warfield,* 2:21–279. Ed. by John E. Meeter. Nutley, N.J.: Presbyterian and Reformed, 1973 (article first published 1896).

Wells, David. *No Place for Truth, or, Whatever Happened to Evangelical Theology?* Grand Rapids: Eerdmans, 1993.

Woodbridge, John D., and Thomas E. McComiskey, eds. *Doing Theology in Today's World: Essays in Honor of Kenneth S. Kantzer.* Grand Rapids: Zondervan, 1991.

SCRIPTURE MEMORY PASSAGE

Students have repeatedly mentioned that one of the most valuable parts of any of their courses in college or seminary has been the Scripture passages they were required to memorize. "I have hidden your word in my heart that I might not sin against you" (Ps. 119:11 NIV). In each chapter, therefore, I have included an appropriate memory passage so that instructors may incorporate Scripture memory into the course requirements wherever possible. (Scripture memory passages at the end of each chapter are taken from the RSV. These same passages in the NIV and NASB may be found in appendix 2.)

Matthew 28:18–20: *And Jesus came and said to them, "All authority in heaven and on earth has been given to me. Go therefore and make disciples of all nations, baptizing them in the name of the Father and of the Son and of the Holy Spirit, teaching them to observe all that I have commanded you; and lo, I am with you always, to the close of the age."*

HYMN

Systematic theology at its best will result in praise. It is appropriate therefore at the end of each chapter to include a hymn related to the subject of that chapter. In a classroom setting, the hymn can be sung together at the beginning or end of class. Alternatively, an individual reader can sing it privately or simply meditate quietly on the words.

For almost every chapter the words of the hymns were found in *Trinity Hymnal* (Philadelphia: Great Commission Publications, 1990),[10] the hymnal of the Presbyterian Church in America and the Orthodox Presbyterian Church, but most of them are found in many other common hymnals. Unless otherwise noted, the words of these hymns are now in public domain and no longer subject to copyright restrictions: therefore they may be freely copied for overhead projector use or photocopied.

Why have I used so many old hymns? Although I personally like many of the more recent worship songs that have come into wide use, when I began to select hymns that would correspond to the great doctrines of the Christian faith, I realized that the great hymns of the church throughout history have a doctrinal richness and breadth that is still unequaled. For several of the chapters in this book, I know of no modern worship song that covers the same subject in an extended way—perhaps this can be a challenge to modern songwriters to study these chapters and then write songs reflecting the teaching of Scripture on the respective subjects.

For this chapter, however, I found no hymn ancient or modern that thanked God for the privilege of studying systematic theology from the pages of Scripture. Therefore I have selected a hymn of general praise, which is always appropriate.

"O for a Thousand Tongues to Sing"

This hymn by Charles Wesley (1707–88) begins by wishing for "a thousand tongues" to sing God's praise. Verse 2 is a prayer that God would "assist me" in singing his praise throughout the earth. The remaining verses give praise to Jesus (vv. 3–6) and to God the Father (v. 7).

> O for a thousand tongues to sing
> My great Redeemer's praise,
> The glories of my God and King,
> The triumphs of His grace.
>
> My gracious Master and my God,
> Assist me to proclaim,
> To spread through all the earth abroad,
> The honors of Thy name.
>
> Jesus! the name that charms our fears,
> That bids our sorrows cease;
> 'Tis music in the sinner's ears,
> 'Tis life and health and peace.
>
> He breaks the pow'r of reigning sin,
> He sets the prisoner free;
> His blood can make the foulest clean;

---

[10] This hymn book is completely revised from a similar hymnal of the same title published by the Orthodox Presbyterian Church in WW 1961.

His blood availed for me.

He speaks and, list'ning to His voice,
New life the dead receive;
The mournful, broken hearts rejoice;
The humble poor believe.

Hear him, ye deaf; his praise, ye dumb,
Your loosened tongues employ,
Ye blind, behold your Savior come;
And leap, ye lame, for joy.

Glory to God and praise and love
Be ever, ever giv'n
By saints below and saints above—
The church in earth and heav'n.

AUTHOR: CHARLES WESLEY, 1739, ALT.

Chapter 2

THE CREATION OF MAN

Why did God create us? How did God make us like himself? How can we please him in everyday living?

EXPLANATION AND SCRIPTURAL BASIS

In this book we focus on the pinnacle of God's creative activity, his creation of human beings, both male and female, to be more like him than anything else he has made. We will consider first God's purpose in creating man and the nature of man as God created him to be (chapters 2–4). Then we will look at the nature of sin and man's disobedience to God (chapter 5). Finally, we will examine the initiation of God's plan for saving man, discussing man's relationship to God in the covenants that God established (chapter 6).

A. The Use of the Word *Man* to Refer to the Human Race

Before discussing the subject matter of this chapter, it is necessary to consider briefly whether it is appropriate to use the word *man* to refer to the entire human race (as in the title for this chapter). Some people today object to ever using the word "man" to refer to the human race in general (including both men and women), because it is claimed that such usage is insensitive to women. Those who make this objection would prefer that we *only* use "gender neutral" terms such as "humanity," "humankind," "human beings," or "persons" to refer to the human race.

After considering this suggestion, I decided to continue to use the word "man" (as well as several of these other terms) to refer to the human race in this book because such usage has divine warrant in Genesis 5, and because I think there is a theological issue at stake. In Genesis 5:1–2 we read, "When God created man, he made him in the likeness of God. Male and female he created them, and he blessed them *and named them Man* when they were created" (cf. Gen. 1:27). The Hebrew term translated "Man" is *'ādām*, the same term used for the name of Adam, and the same term that is sometimes used of man in distinction from woman (Gen. 2:22, 25; 3:12; Eccl. 7:28). Therefore the practice of using the same term to refer (1) to male human beings and (2) to the human race generally is a practice that originated with God himself, and we should not find it objectionable or insensitive.

Someone might object that this is just an accidental feature of the Hebrew language, but this argument is not persuasive because Genesis 5:2 specifically describes God's activity of choosing a name that would apply to the human race as a whole.

I am *not* here arguing that we must always duplicate biblical patterns of speech, *or that* it is wrong to use gender-neutral terms sometimes to refer to the human race (as I just did in this sentence), but rather that God's *naming* activity reported in Genesis 5:2 indicates that the use of "man" to refer to the entire race is a good and very appropriate choice, and one that we should not avoid.[1]

The theological issue is whether there is a suggestion of male leadership or headship in the family from the beginning of creation. The fact that God did not choose to call the human race "woman," but "man," probably has some significance for understanding God's original plan for men and women.[2] Of course, this question of the name we use to refer to the race is not the only factor in that discussion, but it is one factor, and our use of language in this regard does have some significance in the discussion of male-female roles today.[3]

B. Why Was Man Created?

1. God Did Not Need to Create Man, Yet He Created Us for His Own Glory. Because of his independence, God does not need us or the rest of creation for anything, yet we and the rest of creation glorify him and bring him joy. Since there was perfect love and fellowship among members of the Trinity for all eternity (John 17:5, 24), God did not create us because he was lonely or because he needed fellowship with other persons—God did not need us for any reason.

Nevertheless, *God created us for his own glory.* In our treatment of his independence we noted that God speaks of his sons and daughters from the ends of the earth as those "whom I created *for my glory*" (Isa. 43:7; cf. Eph. 1:11–12). Therefore, we are to "do all to the glory of God" (1 Cor. 10:31).

This fact guarantees that our lives are significant. When we first realize that God did not need to create us and does not need us for anything, we could conclude that our lives have no importance at all. But Scripture tells us that we were created to glorify God, indicating that we are important *to God himself.* This is the final definition of genuine importance or

---

[1]However, the question of whether to use "man" to refer to a person indefinitely, as in, "If any *man* would come after me, let him deny himself and take up his cross daily and follow me" (Luke 9:23), is a different question, because the naming of the human race is not in view. In these cases, considerateness toward women as well as men, and present-day language patterns, would make it appropriate to use gender-neutral language such as, "If any *one* would come after me."

[2]See chapter 3, p. 56; also Raymond C. Ortlund, Jr., "Male-Female Equality and Male Headship: Genesis 1–3," in *Recovering Biblical Manhood and Womanhood: A Response to Evangelical Feminism,* ed. John Piper and Wayne Grudem (Wheaton, Ill.: Crossway, 1991), p. 98.

[3]This is probably also recognized by many of those who raise the most objection to the use of "man" to refer to the race (namely, feminists who oppose any unique male headship in the family).

significance to our lives: If we are truly important to God for all eternity, then what greater measure of importance or significance could we want?

2. What Is Our Purpose in Life? The fact that God created us for his own glory determines the correct answer to the question, "What is our purpose in life?" Our purpose must be to fulfill the reason that God created us: to glorify him. When we are speaking with respect to God himself, that is a good summary of our purpose. But when we think of our own interests, we make the happy discovery that we are to enjoy God and take delight in him and in our relationship to him. Jesus says, "I came that they may have life, and have it abundantly" (John 10:10). David tells God, "In your presence there is *fulness of joy,* in your right hand are pleasures for evermore" (Ps. 16:11). He longs to dwell in the house of the Lord forever, "to behold the beauty of the Lord" (Ps. 27:4), and Asaph cries out,

> Whom have I in heaven but you?
> > And there is nothing upon earth that I desire besides you.
> My flesh and my heart may fail,
> > but God is the strength of my heart
> > and my portion for ever. (Ps. 73:25–26)

Fullness of joy is found in knowing God and delighting in the excellence of his character. To be in his presence, to enjoy fellowship with him, is a greater blessing than anything that can be imagined.

> How lovely is your dwelling place,
> > O Lord of hosts!
> My soul longs, yea, faints
> > for the courts of the Lord;
> my heart and flesh sing for joy
> > to the living God. . . .
>
> For a day in your courts is better
> > than a thousand elsewhere. (Ps. 84:1–2, 10)

Therefore, the normal heart attitude of a Christian is rejoicing in the Lord and in the lessons of the life he gives us (Rom. 5:2–3; Phil. 4:4; 1 Thess. 5:16–18; James 1:2; 1 Peter 1:6, 8, et al.).[4]

As we glorify God and enjoy him, Scripture tells us that he rejoices in us. We read, "As the bridegroom rejoices over the bride, *so shall your God rejoice over you*" (Isa. 62:5), and Zephaniah prophesies that the Lord "will rejoice over you with gladness, he will renew you in his love; he will exult over you with loud singing as on a day of festival" (Zeph. 3:17–18).

This understanding of the doctrine of the creation of man has very practical results. When we realize that God created us to glorify him, and when we start to act in ways that

---

[4]The first question in the Westminster Larger Catechism is "What is the chief and highest end of man?" The answer is, "Man's chief and highest end is to glorify God, and fully to enjoy Him forever."

fulfill that purpose, then we begin to experience an intensity of joy in the Lord that we have never before known. When we add to that the realization that God himself is rejoicing in our fellowship with him, our joy becomes "inexpressible and filled with heavenly glory" (1 Peter 1:8, author's expanded paraphrase).[5]

Someone might object that it is wrong for God to seek glory for himself in creating man. Certainly it is wrong for human beings to seek glory for themselves, as we see in the dramatic example of the death of Herod Agrippa I. When he proudly accepted the shout of the crowd, "The voice of a god, and not of man!" (Acts 12:22), "immediately an angel of the Lord smote him, because he did not give God the glory; and he was eaten by worms and died" (Acts 12:23). Herod died because he robbed God of glory, glory that God deserved and he did not.

But when God takes glory to himself, from whom is he robbing glory? Is there anyone who deserves glory more than he does? Certainly not! He is the Creator, he made all things, and he *deserves* all glory. He is *worthy* of receiving glory. *Man* may not seek glory for himself, but in this case what is wrong for man is right for God, because he is the Creator. It is *right,* not wrong, that he be glorified—in fact, if he did not receive glory from all creatures in the universe, that would be horribly wrong! The twenty-four elders around God's throne continually sing,

> "You are *worthy,* our Lord and God,
> *to receive glory* and honor and power,
> for you created all things,
> and by your will they existed and were created."
>
> (Rev. 4:11)

Paul exclaims, "For from him and through him and to him are all things. To him be glory for ever. Amen" (Rom. 11:36). When we begin to appreciate the nature of God as the infinitely perfect Creator who deserves all praise, then our hearts will not rest until we give him glory with all of our "heart . . . soul . . . mind, and . . . strength" (Mark 12:30).

C. Man in the Image of God

1. The Meaning of "Image of God." Out of all the creatures God made, only one creature, man, is said to be made "in the image of God."[6] What does that mean? We may use the following definition: *The fact that man is in the image of God means that man is like God and represents God.*

When God says, "Let us make man in our image, after our likeness" (Gen. 1:26), the meaning is that God plans to make a creature similar to himself. Both the Hebrew word for "image" (*tselem*) and the Hebrew word for "likeness" (*demût*) refer to something that is *similar* but not identical to the thing it represents or is an "image" of. The word *image* can also be used of something that *represents* something else.[7]

---

[5]See W. Grudem, *1 Peter,* TNTC (Downers Grove, Ill.: InterVarsity Press, 1990), p. 66.

[6]The Latin phrase *imago Dei* means "image of God" and is sometimes used in theological discussions in place of the English phrase "image of God." I have not used it elsewhere in this book.

Theologians have spent much time attempting to specify one characteristic of man, or a very few, in which the image of God is primarily seen.[8] Some have thought that the image of God consists in man's intellectual ability, others in his power to make moral decisions and willing choices. Others have thought that the image of God referred to man's original moral purity, or his creation as male and female (see Gen. 1:27), or his dominion over the earth.

In this discussion it would be best to focus attention primarily on the *meanings* of the words "image" and "likeness." As we have seen, these terms had quite clear meanings to the original readers. When we realize that the Hebrew words for "image" and "likeness" simply informed the original readers that man was *like* God, and would in many ways *represent* God, much of the controversy over the meaning of "image of God" is seen to be a search for too narrow and too specific a meaning. When Scripture reports that God said, "Let us make man in our image, after our likeness" (Gen. 1:26), it simply would have meant to the original readers, "Let us make man to be *like* us and to *represent* us."

Because "image" and "likeness" had these meanings, Scripture does not need to say something like,

> The fact that man is in the image of God means that man is like God in the following ways: intellectual ability, moral purity, spiritual nature, dominion over the earth, creativity, ability to make ethical choices, and immortality [or some similar statement].

Such an explanation is unnecessary, not only because the terms had clear meanings, but also because no such list could do justice to the subject: the text only needs to affirm that man is *like God,* and the rest of Scripture fills in more details to explain this. In fact, as we read the rest of Scripture, we realize that a full understanding of man's likeness to God would require a full understanding of *who God is* in his being and in his actions and a full understanding of *who man is* and what he does. The more we know about God and man the more similarities we will recognize, and the more fully we will understand what Scripture

---

[7]The word *image* (*tselem*) means an object similar to something else and often representative of it. The word is used to speak of statues or replicas of tumors and of mice (1 Sam. 6:5, 11), of paintings of soldiers on the wall (Ezek. 23:14), and of pagan idols or statues representing deities (Num. 33:42; 2 Kings 11:18; Ezek. 7:20; 16:17, et al.).

The word *likeness* (*demût*) also means an object similar to something else, but it tends to be used more frequently in contexts where the idea of similarity is emphasized more than the idea of being a representative or substitute (of a god, for example). King Ahaz's model or drawing of the altar he saw in Damascus is called a "likeness" (2 Kings 16:10), as are the figures of bulls beneath the bronze altar (2 Chron. 4:3–4), and the wall paintings of Babylonian chariot officers (Ezek. 23:15). In Ps. 58:4 (Heb. v. 5) the venom of the wicked is a "likeness" of the venom of a snake: here the idea is that they are very similar in their characteristics, but there is no thought of actual representation or substitution.

All of this evidence indicates that the English words *image* and *likeness* are very accurate equivalents for the Hebrew terms they translate.

[8]A brief survey of various views is found in D. J. A. Clines, "The Image of God in Man," *TB* (1968), pp. 54–61. Millard Erickson, *Christian Theology* (Grand Rapids: Baker, 1983–85), pp. 498–510, also gives a helpful summary of three major views of the image of God in man that have been held throughout the history of the church: (1) the substantive view, which identifies some particular quality of man (such as reason or spirituality) as being the image of God in man (Luther, Calvin, many early church writers); (2) relational views, which held that the image of God had to do with our interpersonal relationships (Emil Brunner; also Karl Barth, who saw the image of God specifically in our being created as male and female); and (3) the functional view, which holds that the image of God has to do with a function we carry out, usually our exercise of dominion over the creation (a Socinian view that is also held by some modern writers such as Norman Snaith and Leonard Verduin).

means when it says that man is in the image of God. The expression refers to every way in which man is like God.

This understanding of what it means that man is created in the image of God is reinforced by the similarity between Genesis 1:26, where God declares his intention to create man in his image and likeness, and Genesis 5:3: "When Adam had lived a hundred and thirty years, he became the father of a son in his own *likeness* [*demût*], after his *image* [*tselem*], and named him Seth." Seth was not identical to Adam, but he was like him in many ways, as a son is like his father. The text simply means that Seth was like Adam. It does not specify any specific number of ways that Seth was like Adam, and it would be overly restrictive for us to assert that one or another characteristic determined the way in which Seth was in Adam's image and likeness. Was it his brown eyes? Or his curly hair? Perhaps it was his athletic prowess, or his serious disposition or even his quick temper? Of course, such speculation would be useless. It is evident that *every* way in which Seth was like Adam would be a part of his likeness to Adam and thus part of his being "in the image" of Adam. Similarly, *every* way in which man is like God is part of his being in the image and likeness of God.

2. The Fall: God's Image Is Distorted but Not Lost. We might wonder whether man could still be thought to be *like God* after he sinned. This question is answered quite early in Genesis where God gives Noah the authority to establish the death penalty for murder among human beings just after the flood: God says "Whoever sheds the blood of man, by man shall his blood be shed; *for God made man in his own image*" (Gen. 9:6). Even though men are sinful, there is still enough likeness to God remaining in them that to murder another person (to "shed blood" is an Old Testament expression for taking a human life) is to attack the part of creation that most resembles God, and it betrays an attempt or desire (if one were able) to attack God himself.[9] Man is still in God's image. The New Testament gives confirmation to this when James 3:9 says that men generally, not just believers, "are made in the likeness of God."

However, since man has sinned, he is certainly not as fully like God as he was before. His moral purity has been lost and his sinful character certainly does not reflect God's holiness. His intellect is corrupted by falsehood and misunderstanding; his speech no longer continually glorifies God; his relationships are often governed by selfishness rather than love, and so forth. Though man is still in the image of God, in every aspect of life *some* parts of that image have been distorted or lost. In short, "God made man upright, but they have sought out many devices" (Eccl. 7:29). After the fall, then, we are still in God's image—we are still like God and we still represent God—but the image of God in us is distorted; we are less fully like God than we were before the entrance of sin.

Therefore it is important that we understand the full meaning of the image of God not simply from observation of human beings as they currently exist, but from the biblical indications of the nature of Adam and Eve when God created them and when all that God

---

[9]For a detailed analysis of this passage, see John Murray, *Principles of Conduct* (Grand Rapids: Eerdmans, 1957), pp. 109–13.

had made was "very good" (Gen. 1:31). The true nature of man in the image of God was also seen in the earthly life of Christ. The full measure of the excellence of our humanity will not be seen again in life on earth until Christ returns and we have obtained all the benefits of the salvation he earned for us.

3. Redemption in Christ: a Progressive Recovering of More of God's Image. Nonetheless, it is encouraging to turn to the New Testament and see that our redemption in Christ means that we can, even in this life, progressively grow into more and more likeness to God. For example, Paul says that as Christians we have a new nature that is "being renewed in knowledge after the image of its creator" (Col. 3:10). As we gain in true understanding of God, his Word, and his world, we begin to think more and more of the thoughts that God himself thinks. In this way we are "renewed in knowledge" and we become more like God in our thinking. This is a description of the ordinary course of the Christian life. So Paul also can say that we "are being changed into his likeness [lit. "image," Gk. *eikōn*] from one degree of glory to another" (2 Cor. 3:18).[10] Throughout this life, as we grow in Christian maturity we grow in greater likeness to God. More particularly, we grow in likeness to Christ in our lives and in our character. In fact, the goal for which God has redeemed us is that we might be "conformed to the image of his Son" (Rom. 8:29) and thus be exactly like Christ in our moral character.

4. At Christ's Return: Complete Restoration of God's Image. The amazing promise of the New Testament is that just as we have been like Adam (subject to death and sin), we shall also be like Christ (morally pure, never subject to death again): "Just as we have borne the image of the man of dust, we shall also bear the image of the man of heaven" (1 Cor. 15:49).[11] The full measure of our creation in the image of God is not seen in the life of Adam who sinned, nor is it seen in our lives now, for we are imperfect. But the New Testament emphasizes that God's purpose in creating man in his image was completely realized in the person of Jesus Christ. He himself "is the image of God" (2 Cor. 4:4 NASB); "He is the image of the invisible God" (Col. 1:15). In Jesus we see human likeness to God as it was intended to be, and it should cause us to rejoice that God has predestined us "to be *conformed to the image of his son*" (Rom. 8:29; cf. 1 Cor. 15:49): "When he appears *we shall be like him*" (1 John 3:2).

5. Specific Aspects of Our Likeness to God. Though we have argued above that it would be difficult to define all the ways in which we are like God, we can nevertheless mention several aspects of our existence that show us to be more like God than all the rest of creation.[12]

---

[10]In this verse Paul specifically says that we are being changed into the image of Christ, but then four verses later he says that Christ is the image of God (2 Cor. 4:4; both verses use *eikōn*).

[11]The New Testament Greek word for "image" (*eikōn*) has a similar meaning to its Old Testament counterpart (see above). It indicates something that is similar to or very much like the thing it represents. One interesting usage is a reference to the picture of Caesar on a Roman coin. Jesus asked the Pharisees, "Whose likeness [Gk. *eikōn*, "image"] and inscription is this?" They replied, "Caesar's" (Matt. 22:20–21). The image both resembles Caesar and represents him. (The Greek word *homoioma*, "likeness," is not used in the New Testament to refer to man in the likeness of God.)

a. Moral Aspects: (1) We are creatures who are morally accountable before God for our actions. Corresponding to that accountability, we have (2) an inner sense of right and wrong that sets us apart from animals (who have little if any innate sense of morality or justice but simply respond from fear of punishment or hope of reward). When we act according to God's moral standards, our likeness to God is reflected in (3) behavior that is holy and righteous before him, but, by contrast, our *un*likeness to God is reflected whenever we sin.

b. Spiritual Aspects: (4) We have not only physical bodies but also immaterial spirits, and we can therefore act in ways that are significant in the immaterial, spiritual realm of existence. This means that we have (5) a spiritual life that enables us to relate to God as persons, to pray and praise him, and to hear him speaking his words to us.[13] No animal will ever spend an hour in intercessory prayer for the salvation of a relative or a friend! Connected with this spiritual life is the fact that we have (6) immortality; we will not cease to exist but will live forever.

c. Mental Aspects: (7) We have an ability to reason and think logically and learn that sets us apart from the animal world. Animals sometimes exhibit remarkable behavior in solving mazes or working out problems in the physical world, but they certainly do not engage in abstract reasoning—there is no such thing as the "history of canine philosophy," for example, nor have any animals since creation developed at all in their understanding of ethical problems or use of philosophical concepts, etc. No group of chimpanzees will ever sit around the table arguing about the doctrine of the Trinity or the relative merits of Calvinism or Arminianism! In fact, even in developing physical and technical skills we are far different from animals: beavers still build the same kind of dams they have built for a thousand generations, birds still build the same kind of nests, and bees still build the same kinds of hives. But we continue to develop greater skill and complexity in technology, in agriculture, in science, and in nearly every field of endeavor.

(8) Our use of complex, abstract language sets us far apart from the animals. I could tell my son, when he was four years old, to go and get the big, red screwdriver from my workbench in the basement. Even if he had never seen it before, he could easily perform the task because he knew meanings of "go," "get," "big," "red," "screwdriver," "workbench," and "basement." He could have done the same for a small, brown hammer or a black bucket beside the workbench or any of dozens of other items that he perhaps had never seen before but could visualize when I described them in a few brief words. No chimpanzee in all history has been able to perform such a task—a task that has not been learned through repetition with reward, but is simply described in words that refer to an item that the hearer has never seen before. Yet four-year-old human beings can do this routinely, and we think nothing of it. Most eight-year-olds can write an understandable letter to their grandparents describing a trip to the zoo, or can move to a foreign country and learn any other language in the world, and we think it entirely normal. But no animal will ever write such a letter to its grandpar-

---

[12]However, angels also share a significant degree of likeness to God in a number of these aspects.

[13]Although it is not a separate aspect of our likeness to God, the fact that we have been redeemed by Christ sets us apart in an absolute way from every other creature God has made. This is a consequence of our being in God's image, and of God's love for us, rather than one part of what it means to be in his image.

ents, or give the past, present, and future of even one French verb, or read a detective story and understand it, or understand the meaning of even one verse from the Bible. Human children do all these things quite readily, and in so doing they show themselves so far superior to the whole animal kingdom that we wonder why people have sometimes thought that we are merely another kind of animal.

(9) Another mental difference between humans and animals is that we have an awareness of the distant future, even an inward sense that we will live beyond the time of our physical death, a sense that gives many people a desire to attempt to be right with God before they die (God "has put eternity into man's mind," Eccl. 3:11).

(10) Our likeness to God is also seen in our human creativity in areas such as art, music, and literature, and in scientific and technological inventiveness. We should not think of such creativity as restricted to world-famous musicians or artists—it is also reflected in a delightful way in the play acting or skits put on by children, in the skill reflected in the cooking of a meal or the decorating of a home or the planting of a garden, and in the inventiveness shown by every human being who "fixes" something that just wasn't working correctly.

The foregoing aspects of likeness to God have been ways in which we differ from animals *absolutely*, not merely in degree. But there are other areas where we differ from animals in significant degree, and these also can show our likeness to God.

(11) In the area of emotions, our likeness to God is seen in a large difference in degree and complexity of emotions. Of course, animals do show some emotions (anyone who has owned a dog can remember evident expressions of joy, sadness, fear of punishment when it has done wrong, anger if another animal invades its "turf," contentment, and affection, for example). But in the complexity of emotions that we experience, once again we are far different than the rest of creation. After watching my son's baseball game, I can simultaneously feel sad that his team lost, happy that he played well, proud that he was a good sport, thankful to God for giving me a son and giving me the joy of watching him grow up, joyful because of the song of praise that has been echoing in my mind all afternoon, and anxious because we are going to be late for dinner! It is very doubtful that an animal experiences anything approaching this complexity of emotional feeling.

d. Relational Aspects: In addition to our unique ability to relate to God (discussed above), there are other relational aspects of being in God's image. (12) Although animals no doubt have some sense of community with each other, the depth of interpersonal harmony experienced in human marriage, in a human family when it functions according to God's principles, and in a church when a community of believers is walking in fellowship with the Lord and with each other, is much greater than the interpersonal harmony experienced by any animals. In our family relationships and in the church, we are also superior to angels, who do not marry or bear children or live in the company of God's redeemed sons and daughters.

(13) In marriage itself we reflect the nature of God in the fact that as men and women we have equality in importance but difference in roles from the time that God created us (see discussion in chapter 3).

(14) Man is like God also in his relationship to the rest of creation. Specifically, man has been given the right to rule over the creation and when Christ returns will even be given authority to sit in judgment over angels (1 Cor. 6:3; Gen. 1:26, 28; Ps. 8:6–8).

e. Physical Aspects: Is there any sense in which our human bodies are also a part of what it means to be made in the image of God? Certainly we should not think that our physical bodies imply that God himself has a body, for "God is spirit" (John 4:24), and it is sin to think of him or to portray him in any way that would imply that he has a material or a physical body (see Ex. 20:4; Ps. 115:3–8; Rom. 1:23). But even though our physical bodies should in no way be taken to imply that God has a physical body, are there still some ways in which our bodies reflect something of God's own character and thereby constitute part of what it means to be created in the image of God? Certainly this is true in some respects. For example, our physical bodies give us the ability to see with our eyes. This is a Godlike quality because God himself sees, and sees far more than we will ever see, although he does not do it with physical eyes like we have. Our ears give us the ability to hear, and this is a Godlike ability, even though God does not have physical ears. Our mouths give us the ability to speak, reflecting the fact that God is a God who speaks. Our senses of taste and touch and smell give us the ability to understand and enjoy God's creation, reflecting the fact that God himself understands and enjoys his creation, though in a far greater sense than we do.

It is important that we recognize that it is *man himself* who is created in the image of God, not just his spirit or his mind. Certainly our physical bodies are a very important part of our existence and, as transformed when Christ returns, they will continue to be part of our existence for all eternity (see 1 Cor. 15:43–45, 51–55). Our bodies therefore have been created by God as suitable instruments to represent in a physical way our human nature, which has been made to be like God's own nature. In fact, almost everything we do is done by means of the use of our physical bodies—our thinking, our moral judgments, our prayer and praise, our demonstrations of love and concern for each other—all are done using the physical bodies God has given us. Therefore, if we are careful to point out that we are *not* saying that God has a physical body, we may say that (15) our physical bodies in various ways reflect something of God's own character as well. Moreover, much physical movement and demonstration of God-given skill comes about through the use of our body. And certainly (16) the God-given physical ability to bear and raise children who are like ourselves (see Gen. 5:3) is a reflection of God's own ability to create human beings who are like himself.

Especially in the last several points, these differences between human beings and the rest of creation are not *absolute differences* but often differences of very great degree. We mentioned that there is some kind of emotion experienced by animals. There is some experience of authority in relationships where animal communities have leaders whose authority is accepted by the others in the group. Moreover, there is *some* similarity even in those differences we think more absolute: animals are able to reason to some extent and can communicate with each other in various ways that in some primitive sense can be called "language." This should not be surprising: if God made the entire creation so that it reflects his character in various ways, this is what we would expect. In fact, the more complex and highly developed animals are *more* like God than lower forms of animals.

Therefore we should not say that *only* man reflects any likeness to God at all, for in one way or another all of creation reflects some likeness to God. But it is still important to recognize that *only man*, out of all of creation, is so like God that he can be said to be "in the image of God." This scriptural affirmation, together with the scriptural commands that we are to imitate God in our lives (Eph. 5:1; 1 Peter 1:16), and the observable facts that we can recognize in looking at ourselves and the rest of creation, all indicate that we are *much more like God* than all the rest of creation. In some respects the differences are absolute, and in other respects they are relative, but they are all significant.

Finally, our appreciation of the ways in which we are like God can be enhanced by the realization that, unlike the rest of God's creation, we have an ability to grow to become *more like God* throughout our lives. Our moral sense can be more highly developed through study of Scripture and prayer. Our moral behavior can reflect more and more the holiness of God (2 Cor. 7:1; 1 Peter 1:16, et al.). Our spiritual life can be enriched and deepened. Our use of reason and language can become more accurate and truthful and more honoring to God. Our sense of the future can become intensified as we grow in our hope of living with God forever. Our future existence can be enriched as we lay up treasures in heaven and seek for increased heavenly reward (see Matt. 6:19–21; 1 Cor. 3:10–15; 2 Cor. 5:10). Our ability to rule over the creation can be extended by faithful use of the gifts God has given us; our faithfulness to the God-given purposes for our creation as men and women can be increased as we follow biblical principles in our families; our creativity can be employed in ways that are more and more pleasing to God; our emotions can be more and more conformed to the pattern of Scripture so that we become more like David, a man after God's own heart (1 Sam. 13:14). Our interpersonal harmony in our families and in the church can reflect more and more the unity that exists among the persons in the Trinity. As we consciously seek to grow into greater likeness to God in all these areas, we also demonstrate an ability that itself sets us apart from the rest of creation.

6. Our Great Dignity as Bearers of God's Image. It would be good for us to reflect on our likeness to God more often. It will probably amaze us to realize that when the Creator of the universe wanted to create something "in his image," something *more like himself* than all the rest of creation, he made us. This realization will give us a profound sense of dignity and significance as we reflect on the excellence of all the rest of God's creation: the starry universe, the abundant earth, the world of plants and animals, and the angelic kingdoms are remarkable, even magnificent. But we are more like our Creator than any of these things. We are the culmination of God's infinitely wise and skillful work of creation. Even though sin has greatly marred that likeness, we nonetheless now reflect much of it and shall even more as we grow in likeness to Christ.

Yet we must remember that even fallen, sinful man has the *status* of being in God's image (see discussion of Gen. 9:6, above). Every single human being, no matter how much the image of God is marred by sin, or illness, or weakness, or age, or any other disability, still has the *status* of being in God's image and therefore must be treated with the dignity and respect that is due to God's image-bearer. This has profound implications for our conduct toward others. It means that people of every race deserve equal dignity and rights. It means that elderly people, those seriously ill, the mentally retarded, and children yet unborn, deserve full protection and honor as human beings. If we ever deny our unique status in creation as God's only image-bearers, we will soon begin to depreciate the value of human life, will tend to see humans as merely a higher form of animal, and will begin to treat others as such. We will also lose much of our sense of meaning in life.

QUESTIONS FOR PERSONAL APPLICATION

1. According to Scripture, what should be the major purpose of your life? If you consider the major commitments or goals of your life at the present time (with respect to friendships, marriage, education, job, use of money, church relationships, etc.), are you acting as though your goal were the one that Scripture specifies? Or do you have some other goals that you have acted upon (perhaps without consciously deciding to do so)? As you think about the pattern of most of your days, do you think that God delights in you and rejoices over you?

2. How does it make you feel to think that you, as a human being, are more like God than any other creature in the universe? How does that knowledge make you want to act?

3. Do you think that there are any more intelligent, more Godlike creatures anywhere else in the universe? What does the fact that Jesus became a man rather than some other kind of creature say about the importance of human beings in God's sight?

4. Do you think that God has made us so that we become more happy or less happy when we grow to become more like him? As you look over the list of ways in which we can be more like God, can you name one or two areas in which growth in likeness to God has given you increasing joy in your life? In which areas would you now like to make more progress in likeness to God?

5. Is it only Christians or all people who are in the image of God? How does that make you feel about your relationships to non-Christians?

6. Do you think an understanding of the image of God might change the way you think and act toward people who are racially different, or elderly, or weak, or unattractive to the world?

SPECIAL TERMS

image of God　　　　　　*imago Dei*　　　　　　likeness

BIBLIOGRAPHY

Barclay, D. R. "Creation." In *NDT,* pp. 177–79.
Berkouwer, G. C. *Man: The Image of God.* Grand Rapids: Eerdmans, 1962.

Boston, Thomas. *Human Nature in Its Fourfold State*. London: Banner of Truth, 1964 (first published 1720).

Ferguson, S. B. "Image of God." In *NDT*, pp. 328–29.

Henry, C. F. H. "Image of God." In *EDT*, pp. 545–48.

Hoekema, Anthony A. *Created in God's Image*. Grand Rapids: Eerdmans, and Exeter: Paternoster, 1986, pp. 1–111.

Hughes, Philip Edgcumbe. *The True Image: The Origin and Destiny of Man in Christ*. Grand Rapids: Eerdmans, and Leicester: Inter-Varsity Press, 1989, pp. 1–70.

Kline, Meredith G. *Images of the Spirit*. Grand Rapids: Baker, 1980.

Laidlaw, John. *The Bible Doctrine of Man*. Edinburgh: T. & T. Clark, 1905.

Machen, J. Gresham. *The Christian View of Man*. London: Banner of Truth, 1965 (reprint of 1937 edition).

McDonald, H. D. "Man, Doctrine of." In *EDT*, pp. 676–80.

_____. *The Christian View of Man*. Westchester, Ill.: Crossway, 1981.

Robinson, H. W. *The Christian Doctrine of Man*. 3d ed. Edinburgh: T. & T. Clark, 1926.

SCRIPTURE MEMORY PASSAGE

Genesis 1:26–27: *Then God said, "Let us make man in our image, after our likeness; and let them have dominion over the fish of the sea, and over the birds of the air, and over the cattle, and over all the earth, and over every creeping thing that creeps upon the earth." So God created man in his own image, in the image of God he created him; male and female he created them.*

HYMNS

"Love Divine, All Love Excelling"

Love divine, all love excelling,
    Joy of heav'n, to earth come down!
Fix in us thy humble dwelling;
    All thy faithful mercies crown.
Jesus, thou art all compassion,
    Pure, unbounded love thou art;
Visit us with thy salvation,
    Enter ev'ry trembling heart.

Breathe, O breathe thy loving Spirit
    Into ev'ry troubled breast!
Let us all in thee inherit,
    Let us find the promised rest.
Take away the love of sinning;
    Alpha and Omega be;
End of faith, as its beginning,
    Set our hearts at liberty.

Come, Almighty to deliver,
    Let us all thy life receive;
Suddenly return, and never,
    Never more thy temples leave.
Thee we would be always blessing,
    Serve thee as thy hosts above,
Pray, and praise thee, without ceasing,
    Glory in thy perfect love.

Finish, then, thy new creation;
    Pure and spotless let us be;
Let us see thy great salvation
    Perfectly restored in thee:
Changed from glory into glory,
    Till in heav'n we take our place,
Till we cast our crowns before thee,
    Lost in wonder, love, and praise.

AUTHOR: CHARLES WESLEY, 1747

Alternative hymn: "Thou Art Worthy"

Thou art worthy, thou art worthy,
    thou art worthy, O Lord.
To receive glory, glory and honor,
    glory and honor and power.
For thou hast created, hast all things created,
    thou hast created all things;
And for thy pleasure, they are created,
    thou art worthy, O Lord.

AUTHOR: PAULINE MICHAEL MILLS
COPYRIGHT C. FRED BOCK MUSIC, 1963, 1975.
USED BY PERMISSION.

Chapter 3

MAN AS MALE AND FEMALE

Why did God create two sexes? Can men and women be equal and yet have different roles?

EXPLANATION AND SCRIPTURAL BASIS

We noted in the previous chapter that one aspect of man's creation in the image of God is his creation as male and female: "So God created man in his own image, in the image of God he created him; *male and female he created them*" (Gen. 1:27). The same connection between creation in the image of God and creation as male and female is made in Genesis 5:1–2, "When God created man, he made him in the likeness of God. *Male and female* he created them, and he blessed them and named them Man when they were created."[1] Although the creation of man as male and female is not the only way in which we are in the image of God, it is a significant enough aspect of our creation in the image of God that Scripture mentions it in the very same verse in which it describes God's initial creation of man. We may summarize the ways in which our creation as male and female represents something of our creation in God's image as follows:

The creation of man as male and female shows God's image in (1) harmonious interpersonal relationships, (2) equality in personhood and importance, and (3) difference in role and authority.[2]

A. Personal Relationships

God did not create human beings to be isolated persons, but, in making us in his image, he made us in such a way that we can attain interpersonal unity of various sorts in all forms of human society. Interpersonal unity can be especially deep in the human family and also

---

[1] On the question of whether to use the English word *man* to refer to human beings generally (both male and female), see chapter 2, pp. 34–35.

[2] For a more extensive discussion of the theological implications of male-female differentiation in Genesis 1–3, see Raymond C. Ortlund, Jr., "Male-Female Equality and Male Headship: Genesis 1–3," in *Recovering Biblical Manhood and Womanhood: A Response to Evangelical Feminism,* ed. by John Piper and Wayne Grudem (Wheaton, Ill.: Crossway, 1991), p. 98. I have depended on Dr. Ortlund's analysis at several points in this chapter.

in our spiritual family, the church. Between men and women, interpersonal unity comes to its fullest expression in this age in marriage, where husband and wife become, in a sense, two persons in one: "Therefore a man leaves his father and his mother and cleaves to his wife, and they become one flesh" (Gen. 2:24). This unity is not only a physical unity; it is also a spiritual and emotional unity of profound dimensions. A husband and wife joined together in marriage are people that "God has joined together" (Matt. 19:6). Sexual union with someone other than one's own wife or husband is a specially offensive kind of sin against one's own body (1 Cor. 6:16, 18–20), and, within marriage, husbands and wives no longer have exclusive rule over their own bodies, but share them with their spouses (1 Cor. 7:3–5). Husbands "should love their wives as their own bodies" (Eph. 5:28). The union between husband and wife is not temporary but lifelong (Mal. 2:14–16; Rom. 7:2), and it is not trivial but is a profound relationship created by God in order to picture the relationship between Christ and his church (Eph. 5:23–32).

The fact that God created two distinct persons as male and female, rather than just one man, is part of our being in the image of God because it can be seen to reflect to some degree the plurality of persons within the Trinity. In the verse prior to the one that tells of our creation as male and female, we see the first explicit indication of a plurality of persons within God: "Then God said, 'Let *us* make man in *our* image, after our likeness; and let them have dominion'" (Gen. 1:26). There is some similarity here: just as there was fellowship and communication and sharing of glory among the members of the Trinity before the world was made (see John 17:5, 24), so God made Adam and Eve in such a way that they would share love and communication and mutual giving of honor to one another in their interpersonal relationship. Of course such reflection of the Trinity would come to expression in various ways within human society, but it would certainly exist from the beginning in the close interpersonal unity of marriage.

Someone might object that such a representation of the plurality of persons in God is not really a complete one, for God is three persons in one while God created Adam and Eve as only two persons in one. If God intended us to reflect the plurality of persons in the Trinity, why did he not create three persons rather than two who could reflect the interpersonal unity among the members of the Trinity? First, we must agree that this fact shows the analogy between marriage and the Trinity to be an inexact one. Second, although we cannot be certain of the reasons why God did not do something when Scripture does not explicitly tell us those reasons, we can suggest two possible answers: (1) The fact that God is three in one while Adam and Eve were only two in one may be a reminder that God's own excellence is far greater than ours, that he possesses far greater plurality and far greater unity than we ourselves, as creatures, can possess. (2) Though the unity is not exactly the same, the unity in a family among husband, wife, and children, does also reflect to some degree the interpersonal unity yet diversity of persons among the members of the Trinity.

A second objection might be raised from the fact that Jesus himself was unmarried, that Paul was unmarried at the time he was an apostle (and perhaps earlier), and that Paul in 1 Corinthians 7:1, 7–9 seems to say that it is better for Christians not to marry. If marriage is such an important part of our reflection of the image of God, then why were Paul and Jesus not married, and why did Paul encourage others not to be married?

For Jesus, the situation is unique, for he is both God and man, and sovereign Lord over all creation. Rather than being married to any one individual human being, he has taken the entire church as his bride (see Eph. 5:23–32) and enjoys with each member of his church a spiritual and emotional unity that will last for eternity.

The situation with Paul and his advice to the Corinthian Christians is somewhat different. There Paul does not say that it is wrong to marry (see 1 Cor. 7:28, 36), but rather views marriage as something good, a right and a privilege that may be given up for the sake of the kingdom of God: "I think that in view of the present distress it is well for a person to remain as he is . . . the appointed time has grown very short. . . . For the form of this world is passing away" (1 Cor. 7:26, 29, 31). In this way Paul gives up one way in which he might reflect likeness to God (marriage) in order to further other ways in which he might reflect likeness to God and further God's purposes in the world (namely, in his work for the church). For example, his evangelism and discipleship are thought of as bearing "spiritual children" and nurturing them in the Lord (see 1 Cor. 4:14, where he calls the Corinthians "my beloved children"; also Gal. 4:19; 1 Tim. 1:2; Titus 1:4). Moreover, the entire building up of the church was a process of bringing thousands of people to glorify God as they reflected his character more fully in their lives. In addition, we must realize that marriage is not the only way in which the unity and diversity in the Trinity can be reflected in our lives. It is also reflected in the union of believers in the fellowship of the church—and in genuine church fellowship, single persons (like Paul and Jesus) as well as those who are married can have interpersonal relationships that reflect the nature of the Trinity. Therefore, building the church and increasing its unity and purity also promote the reflection of God's character in the world.

B. Equality in Personhood and Importance

Just as the members of the Trinity are equal in their importance and in their full existence as distinct persons, so men and women have been created by God to be equal in their importance and personhood. When God created man, he created both "male and female" in his image (Gen. 1:27; 5:1–2). Men and women are made *equally in God's image,* and both men and women reflect God's character in their lives. This means that we should see aspects of God's character reflected in each other's lives. If we lived in a society consisting of only Christian men or a society consisting of only Christian women, we would not gain as full a picture of the character of God as when we see both godly men and godly women in their complementary differences together reflecting the beauty of God's character.

But if we are equally in God's image, then certainly men and women are *equally important* to God and *equally valuable* to him. We have equal worth before him for all eternity. The fact that both men and women are said by Scripture to be "in the image of God" should exclude all feelings of pride or inferiority and any idea that one sex is "better" or "worse" than the other. In particular, in contrast to many non-Christian cultures and religions, no one should feel proud or superior because he is a man, and no one should feel disappointed or inferior because she is a woman.[3] If God thinks us to be equal in value, then that settles the question, for God's evaluation is the true standard of personal value for all eternity.

---

[3] In the past decade news agencies have reported a common practice in China whereby parents of a newborn daughter will often leave her to die in order that they might try again to have a son under China's strict "one couple, one child" policy.

When in 1 Corinthians 11:7 Paul says, "A man ought not to cover his head, since he is the image and glory of God; but woman is the glory of man," he is not denying that woman was created in the image of God. He is simply saying that there are abiding differences between men and women that should be reflected in the way they dress and act in the assembled congregation. One of those differences is that man in relationship to woman has a particular role of representing God or showing what he is like, and woman in that relationship shows the excellence of the man from whom she was created. Yet in both cases Paul goes on to emphasize their interdependence (see vv. 11–12).

Our equality as persons before God, reflecting the equality of persons in the Trinity, should lead naturally to men and women giving honor to one another. Proverbs 31 is a beautiful picture of the honor given to a godly woman:

> A good wife who can find?
> > She is far more precious than jewels....
> Her children rise up and call her blessed;
> > her husband also, and he praises her:
> "Many women have done excellently,
> > but you surpass them all."
> Charm is deceitful, and beauty is vain,
> > but a woman who fears the LORD is to be praised.
> > > (Prov. 31:10, 28–30)

Similarly, Peter tells husbands that they are to "bestow honor" on their wives (1 Peter 3:7), and Paul emphasizes, "In the Lord woman is not independent of man nor man of woman; for as woman was made from man, so man is now born of woman" (1 Cor. 11:11, 12). Both men and women are equally important; both depend upon each other; both are worthy of honor.

The equality in personhood with which men and women were created is emphasized in a new way in the new covenant church. At Pentecost we see the fulfillment of Joel's prophecy in which God promises:

> "I will pour out my Spirit upon all flesh,
> and your *sons* and your *daughters* shall prophesy
> ... and on my *menservants* and my *maidservants* in those days
> I will pour out my Spirit; and they shall prophesy."
> > (Acts 2:17–18; quoting Joel 2:28–29)

The Holy Spirit is poured out in new power on the church, and men and women *both* are given gifts to minister in remarkable ways. Spiritual gifts are distributed to all men and women, beginning at Pentecost and continuing throughout the history of the church. Paul regards every Christian as a valuable member of the body of Christ, for "to *each* is given the manifestation of the Spirit for the common good" (1 Cor. 12:7). After mentioning several

---

In contrast to the biblical view of equality in importance for men and women, such a tragic practice not only results in much loss of innocent human life, but also proclaims loudly to every woman in that society that she is less valuable than a man. (In other societies parents who secretly think that it is better to have a baby boy than a baby girl also show that they have not fully understood the biblical teaching on the fact that women and men are fully equal in value in God's sight.)

gifts he says, "All these are inspired by one and the same Spirit, who apportions *to each one* individually as he wills," (1 Cor. 12:11). Peter also, in writing to many churches throughout Asia Minor, says, "As *each* has received a gift, employ it for one another, as good stewards of God's varied grace" (1 Peter 4:10). These texts do not teach that all believers have the same gifts, but they do mean that both men and women will have valuable gifts for the ministry of the church, and that we should expect that these gifts will be widely and freely distributed to both men and women.

It seems, therefore, pointless to ask, "Who can pray more effectively, men or women?" or, "Who can sing praise to God better, men or women?" or, "Who will have more spiritual sensitivity and depth of relationship with God?" To all of these questions, we simply cannot give an answer. Men and women are equal in their ability to receive the new covenant empowerment of the Holy Spirit. There have been both great men and great women of God throughout the history of the church. Both men and women have been mighty warriors in prayer, prevailing over earthly powers and kingdoms and spiritual strongholds in the authority of our Lord Jesus Christ.[4]

Equality before God is further emphasized in the new covenant church in the ceremony of baptism. At Pentecost, both men and women who believed were baptized: "those who received his word were baptized, and there were added that day about three thousand souls" (Acts 2:41). This is significant because in the old covenant, the sign of membership of God's people was circumcision, which was given only to men. The new sign of membership of God's people, the sign of baptism, given to both men and women, is further evidence that both should be seen as fully and equally members of the people of God.

Equality in status among God's people is also emphasized by Paul in Galatians: "For as many of you as were baptized into Christ have put on Christ. There is neither Jew nor Greek, there is neither slave nor free, *there is neither male nor female;* for you are all one in Christ Jesus" (Gal. 3:27–28). Paul is here underlining the fact that no class of people, such as the Jewish people who had come from Abraham by physical descent, or the freedmen who had greater economic and legal power, could claim special status or privilege in the church. Slaves should not think themselves inferior to free men or women, nor should the free think themselves superior to slaves. Jews should not think themselves superior to Greeks, nor should Greeks think themselves inferior to Jews. Similarly, Paul wants to ensure that men will not adopt some of the attitudes of the surrounding culture, or even some of the attitudes of first-century Judaism, and think that they have greater importance than women or are of superior value before God. Nor should women think themselves inferior or less important in the church. Both men and women, Jews and Greeks, slaves and free, are equal in importance and value to God and equal in membership in Christ's body, the church, for all eternity.

---

[4]Perhaps the answer to the questions, "Who can pray better?" and "Who can praise God better?" should be "both together." Although there is much value in a men's prayer meeting or in a gathering of women for prayer, there is nothing richer and more complete than the whole fellowship of God's people, both men and women, and even their children who are old enough to understand and participate, gathered together before God's throne in prayer: "When the day of Pentecost had come, they *were all together in one place*" (Acts 2:1). "And when they heard it, they lifted their voices *together* to God" (Acts 4:24). Peter "went to the house of Mary, the mother of John whose other name was Mark, where *many were gathered together* and were praying" (Acts 12:12).

CHAPTER 3 · MAN AS MALE AND FEMALE

In practical terms, we must never think that there are any second-class citizens in the church. Whether someone is a man or woman, employer or employee, Jew or Gentile, black or white, rich or poor, healthy or ill, strong or weak, attractive or unattractive, extremely intelligent or slow to learn, all are equally valuable to God and should be equally valuable to one another as well. This equality is an amazing and wonderful element of the Christian faith and sets Christianity apart from almost all religions and societies and cultures. The true dignity of godly manhood and womanhood can be fully realized only in obedience to God's redeeming wisdom as found in Scripture.

C. Differences in Roles

1. The Relationship Between the Trinity and Male Headship in Marriage. Between the members of the Trinity there has been equality in importance, personhood, and deity throughout all eternity. But there have also been differences in roles between the members of the Trinity. God the Father has always been the Father and has always related to the Son as a Father relates to his Son. Though all three members of the Trinity are equal in power and in all other attributes, the Father has a greater authority. He has a leadership role among all the members of the Trinity that the Son and Holy Spirit do not have. In creation, the Father speaks and initiates, but the work of creation is carried out through the Son and sustained by the continuing presence of the Holy Spirit (Gen. 1:1–2; John 1:1–3; 1 Cor. 8:6; Heb. 1:2). In redemption, the Father sends the Son into the world, and the Son comes and is obedient to the Father and dies to pay for our sins (Luke 22:42; Phil. 2:6–8). After the Son has ascended into heaven, the Holy Spirit comes to equip and empower the church (John 16:7; Acts 1:8; 2:1–36). The Father did not come to die for our sins, nor did the Holy Spirit. The Father was not poured out on the church at Pentecost in new covenant power, nor was the Son. Each member of the Trinity has distinct roles or functions. Differences in roles and authority between the members of the Trinity are thus completely consistent with equal importance, personhood, and deity.

If human beings are to reflect the character of God, then we would expect some similar differences in roles among human beings, even with respect to the most basic of all differences among human beings, the difference between male and female. And this is certainly what we find in the biblical text.

Paul makes this parallel explicit when he says, "I want you to understand that the head of every man is Christ, *the head of a woman is her husband,* and *the head of Christ is God*" (1 Cor. 11:3). Here is a distinction in authority that may be represented as in figure 3.1.

Just as God the Father has authority over the Son, though the two are equal in deity, so in a marriage, the husband has authority over the wife, though they are equal in personhood.[5] In this case, the man's role is like that of God the Father, and the woman's role is parallel to that of God the Son. They are equal in importance, but they have different roles. In the context of 1 Corinthians 11:2–16, Paul sees this as a basis for telling the Corinthians to

---

[5]Some have suggested that the word "head" in 1 Cor. 11:3 means "source" and has nothing to do with authority in marriage. For example, when referring to Paul's use of the word "head" to say that "the head of every man is Christ, the head of woman is her husband, and the head of Christ is God" (1 Cor. 11:3), Gordon Fee says that "Paul's understanding of the metaphor, therefore, and almost certainly the only one the Corinthians would have grasped, is 'head' as 'source,' especially 'source

wear the different kinds of clothing appropriate for the men and women of that day, so that the distinctions between men and women might be outwardly evident in the Christian assembly.[6]

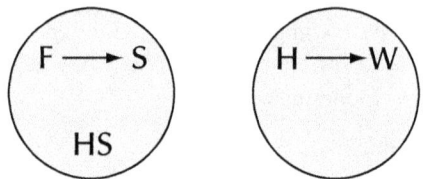

EQUALITY AND DIFFERENCES IN THE TRINITY ARE REFLECTED
IN EQUALITY AND DIFFERENCES IN MARRIAGE
Figure 3.1

2. Indications of Distinct Roles Before the Fall. But were these distinctions between male and female roles part of God's original creation, or were they introduced as part of the punishment of the fall? When God told Eve, "Yet your desire shall be for your husband, and *he shall rule over you*" (Gen. 3:16), was that the time when Eve began to be subject to Adam's authority?

The idea that differences in authority were introduced only after there was sin in the world has been advocated by several writers such as Aida B. Spencer[7] and Gilbert Bilezikian.[8] Bilezikian says, "Because it resulted from the Fall, the rule of Adam over Eve is viewed as satanic in origin, no less than is death itself."[9]

---

of life'-" (*The First Epistle to the Corinthians*, NIC [Grand Rapids: Eerdmans, 1987], p. 503).

Similarly, the statement, "Men, Women and Biblical Equality," published as an advertisement in *CT*, April 9, 1990, pp. 36–37, says, "The husband's function as 'head' is to be understood as self-giving love and service within this relationship of mutual submission (Eph. 5:21–33; Col. 3:19; 1 Pet. 3:7)" (p. 1, para. 11). Thus they understand "head" to mean "source" (of love and service), not "authority over."

For a response to this interpretation and a discussion of reasons why the word "head" here must mean "authority over," not "source," see W. Grudem, "Does *Kephalē* ('Head') Mean 'Source' or 'Authority Over' in Greek Literature? A Survey of 2,336 Examples," *TrinJ* 6, n.s. (Spring 1985), pp. 38–59, and W. Grudem, "The Meaning of *Kephalē* ('Head'): A Response to Recent Studies," *TrinJ* 11, n.s. (Spring 1990), pp. 3–72 (reprinted in *Recovering Biblical Manhood and Womanhood: A Response to Evangelical Feminism*, pp. 425–68). See also Joseph Fitzmyer, "Another Look at *Kephalē* in 1 Cor. 11:3," *NTS* 35 (1989), pp. 503–11. Even in the few examples where people have claimed that "head" could mean "source" when applied to a person, the person is *always* one in authority. No counter-examples to this have ever been found in ancient Greek literature.

[6]The fact that head coverings were the kind of clothing that distinguished women from men in first-century Corinth meant that Paul directed the women to wear head coverings in church. But this does not mean that women should wear head coverings in societies where that is not a distinctive sign of being a woman. The contemporary application would be that women should dress to look like women and men should dress to look like men, in whatever form those clothing patterns are expressed in each society: Paul is not in favor of unisex clothing! For further discussion, see Thomas R. Schreiner, "Head Coverings, Prophecies and the Trinity: 1 Corinthians 11:2–16," in *Recovering Biblical Manhood and Womanhood*, pp. 124–39.

[7]*Beyond the Curse*, 2d ed. (Nashville: Thomas Nelson, 1985), pp. 20–42.

[8]*Beyond Sex Roles* (Grand Rapids: Baker, 1985), pp. 21–58.
[9]Ibid., p. 58.

[10]Some object that this would not be appropriate in the Genesis narrative, for animals were created before Adam, and

However, if we examine the text of the creation narrative in Genesis, we see several indications of *differences in role* between Adam and Eve *even before there was sin in the world.*

a. Adam Was Created First, Then Eve: The fact that God first created Adam, then after a period of time created Eve (Gen. 2:7, 18–23), suggests that God saw Adam as having a leadership role in his family. No such two-stage procedure is mentioned for any of the animals God made, but here it seems to have a special purpose. The creation of Adam first is consistent with the Old Testament pattern of "primogeniture," the idea that the firstborn in any generation in a human family has leadership in the family for that generation. The right of primogeniture is assumed throughout the Old Testament text, even when at times because of God's special purposes the birthright is sold or otherwise transferred to a younger person (Gen. 25:27–34; 35:23; 38:27–30; 49:3–4; Deut. 21:15–17; 1 Chron. 5:1–2). The "birthright" belongs to the firstborn son and is his unless special circumstances intervene to change that fact.[10] The fact that we are correct in seeing a purpose of God in creating Adam first, and that this purpose reflects an abiding distinction in the roles God has given to men and women, is supported by 1 Timothy 2:13, where Paul uses the fact that "Adam was formed first, then Eve" as a reason for restricting some distinct governing and teaching roles in the church to men.

b. Eve Was Created as a Helper for Adam: Scripture specifies that God made Eve for Adam, not Adam for Eve. God said, "It is not good that the man should be alone; *I will make him a helper fit for him*" (Gen. 2:18). Paul sees this as significant enough to base a requirement for differences between men and women in worship on it. He says, "Neither was man created for woman, but *woman for man*" (1 Cor. 11:9). This should not be taken to imply lesser importance, but it does indicate that there was a difference in roles from the beginning.

Recently some writers have denied that the creation of Eve as a helper fit for Adam signals any difference in role or authority, because the word *helper* (Heb., *'ezer*) is often used in the Old Testament of someone who is greater or more powerful than the one who is being helped.[11] In fact, the word *helper* is used in the Old Testament of God himself who helps his people. But the point is that whenever someone "helps" someone else, whether in the Hebrew Old Testament or in our modern-day use of the word *help,* in the specific task in view the person who is helping is occupying a subordinate or inferior position with regard to the person being helped. That is true even when I "help" a young boy in my neighborhood to fix his bicycle—it is his responsibility, and his task, and I am only giving some assistance as needed; it is not my responsibility. David Clines concludes that this is the case throughout the Hebrew Old Testament:

> What I conclude, from viewing all of the occurrences in the Hebrew Bible, is that though superiors may help inferiors, strong may help weak, gods may help humans, in the act of helping they are being "inferior." That is to say, they are

---

this would give animals the authority to rule over humans (so Bilezikian, *Beyond Sex Roles,* p. 257, n. 13). But this objection fails to understand that the principle of primogeniture only occurs among human beings and is, in fact, limited to those in the same family. (Bilezikian raises other objections [pp. 255–57] but fails to deal with the New Testament endorsement of this understanding of Gen. 2 in 1 Tim. 2:13.)

[11]See Aida B. Spencer, *Beyond the Curse,* pp. 23–29.

[12]David J. A. Clines, "What Does Eve Do to Help? and Other Irredeemably Androcentric Orientations in Genesis 1–3," paper

subjecting themselves to a secondary, subordinate position. Their help may be necessary or crucial, but they are assisting some task that is someone else's responsibility. They are not actually doing the task themselves, or even in cooperation, for there is different language for that. Being a helper is not a Hebrew way of being an equal.[12]

Another objection is that the Hebrew term translated "fit for" in Genesis 2:18 implies that Eve was actually superior to Adam, because the term really means "in front of."[13] But Raymond C. Ortlund correctly points out that the Hebrew term cannot mean "superior to" or Psalm 119:168 would have the psalmist saying to God, "All my ways are *superior* to you"! It simply means "corresponding to."[14]

c. Adam Named Eve: The fact that Adam gave names to all the animals (Gen. 2:19–20) indicated Adam's authority over the animal kingdom, because in Old Testament thought the right to name someone implied authority over that person (this is seen both when God gives names to people such as Abraham and Sarah, and when parents give names to their children). Since a Hebrew name designated the character or function of someone, Adam was specifying the characteristics or functions of the animals he named. Therefore when Adam named Eve by saying, "She shall be called Woman, because she was taken out of Man" (Gen. 2:23), it indicated a leadership role on his part as well.[15] This is true before the fall, where Adam names his wife "Woman," and it is true after the fall as well, when "the man called his wife's name Eve, because she was the mother of all living" (Gen. 3:20).[16] Some have objected that Adam doesn't really name Eve before the fall.[17] But certainly calling his wife "Woman" (Gen. 2:23), just as he called all the living creatures by their names (Gen. 2:19–20), is giving her a name. The fact that mothers sometimes give their children names in the Old Testament does not contradict the idea of name-giving as representing authority, since both mothers and fathers have parental authority over their children.

d. God Named the Human Race "Man," Not "Woman": The fact that God named the human race "man," rather than "woman" or some gender-neutral term was explained in chapter 2.[18] Genesis 5:2 specifies that "in the day when they were created" (NASB) God *"named them Man."* The naming of the human race with a term that also referred to Adam in particular, or man in distinction from woman, suggests a leadership role belonging to the man. This is similar to the custom of a woman taking the last name of the man when she marries: it signifies his headship in the family.

---

read at Society of Biblical Literature annual meeting Dec. 7, 1987, in Boston, Massachusetts.

[13]So Aida Spencer, *Beyond the Curse,* pp. 23–26. She says, "The Hebrew text even signifies that the woman is 'in front of' the man or 'over' him!" (p. 26).

[14]Ortlund, "Male-Female Equality," pp. 103–4; cf. BDB, p. 617, 2a.

[15]See the discussion in Ortlund, "Male-Female Equality," pp. 102–3.

[16]Gerhard von Rad says, "Let us remind ourselves once more that name-giving in the ancient Orient was primarily an exercise of sovereignty, of command" (*Genesis: A Commentary,* rev. ed. [Philadelphia: Westminster, 1972], p. 83).

[17]See Bilezikian, *Beyond Sex Roles,* pp. 260–61.

[18]See pp. 34–35.

[19]See Susan T. Foh, "What is the Woman's Desire?" in *WTJ,* vol. 37 (1975), pp. 376–83. Foh notes that this same Hebrew word

e. The Serpent Came to Eve First: Satan, after he had sinned, was attempting to distort and undermine everything that God had planned and created as good. It is likely that Satan (in the form of a serpent), in approaching Eve first, was attempting to institute a role reversal by tempting Eve to take the leadership in disobeying God (Gen. 3:1). This stands in contrast to the way God approached them, for when God spoke to them, he spoke to Adam first (Gen. 2:15–17; 3:9). Paul seems to have this role reversal in mind when he says, "Adam was not deceived, but the woman was deceived and became a transgressor" (1 Tim. 2:14). This at least suggests that Satan was trying to undermine the pattern of male leadership that God had established in the marriage by going first to the woman.

f. God Spoke to Adam First After the Fall: Just as God spoke to Adam on his own even before Eve was created (Gen. 2:15–17), so, after the fall, even though Eve had sinned first, God *came first to Adam* and called *him* to account for his actions: "But the LORD *God called to the man,* and said to *him,* 'Where are you?'" (Gen. 3:9). God thought of Adam as the leader of his family, the one to be called to account first for what had happened in the family. It is significant that though this is after sin has occurred, it is before the statement to Eve, "He shall rule over you" in Genesis 3:16, where some writers today claim male headship in the family began.

g. Adam, Not Eve, Represented the Human Race: Even though Eve sinned first (Gen. 3:6), we are counted sinful because of Adam's sin, not because of Eve's sin. The New Testament tells us, "*In Adam* all die" (1 Cor 15:22; cf. v. 49), and, "Many died through *one man's* trespass" (Rom. 5:15; cf. vv. 12–21). This indicates that God had given Adam headship or leadership with respect to the human race, a role that was not given to Eve.

h. The Curse Brought a Distortion of Previous Roles, Not the Introduction of New Roles: In the punishments God gave to Adam and Eve, he did not introduce new roles or functions, but simply introduced pain and distortion into the functions they previously had. Thus, Adam would still have primary responsibility for tilling the ground and raising crops, but the ground would bring forth "thorns and thistles" and in the sweat of his face he would eat bread (Gen. 3:18, 19). Similarly, Eve would still have the responsibility of bearing children, but to do so would become painful: "In pain you shall bring forth children" (Gen. 3:16). Then God also introduced conflict and pain into the previously harmonious relationship between Adam and Eve. God said to Eve, "Your *desire* shall be *for your husband,* and he shall rule over you" (Gen. 3:16). Susan Foh has effectively argued that the word translated "desire" (Heb. *teshûqāh*) means "desire to conquer," and that it indicates Eve would have a wrongful desire to usurp authority over her husband.[19] If this occurs in a closely parallel statement just a few verses later, when God says to Cain, "Sin is crouching at the door, and its *desire* is for you, but you must master it" (Gen. 4:7 NASB). The parallelism in the Hebrew text between the verses is quite remarkable: six words (counting conjunctions and prepositions) are exactly the same, and in the same order. Another four nouns and pronouns are in the same position and have the same function in the sentence, but they differ only because the parties involved are different. But in that sentence the "desire" that sin has for Cain is surely a *desire to overcome or conquer him,* as is evident from the image of an animal "crouching" at the door waiting for him. The only other example of this Hebrew word is found in Song of Sol. 7:10, where its meaning is unclear but where the sense "desire to have mastery over" is possible (note the progression in Song of Sol. 2:16; 6:3; 7:10). I have been unable to find any other occurrences of this word in ancient Hebrew literature, though Foh does point to some par-

understanding of the word "desire" is correct, as it seems to be, then it would indicate that God is introducing *a conflict into the relationship* between Adam and Eve and a desire on Eve's part to rebel against Adam's authority.

Concerning Adam, God told Eve, "He shall *rule* over you" (Gen. 3:16). Here the word "rule" (Heb. *māshal*) is a strong term usually used of monarchical governments, not generally of authority within a family.[20] The word certainly does not imply any "participatory" government by those who are ruled, but rather has nuances of dictatorial or absolute, uncaring use of authority, rather than considerate, thoughtful rule. It suggests harshness rather than kindness. The sense here is that Adam will misuse his authority *by ruling harshly* over his wife, again introducing pain and conflict into a relationship that was previously harmonious. It is not that Adam had no authority before the fall; it is simply that he will misuse it after the fall.

So in both cases, the curse brought a *distortion* of Adam's humble, considerate leadership and Eve's intelligent, willing submission to that leadership which existed before the fall.

i. Redemption in Christ Reaffirms the Creation Order: If the previous argument about the distortion of roles introduced at the fall is correct, then what we would expect to find in the New Testament is an undoing of the painful aspects of the relationship that resulted from sin and the curse. We would expect that in Christ, redemption would encourage wives not to rebel against their husbands' authority and would encourage husbands not to use their authority harshly. In fact, that is indeed what we do find: "Wives, *be subject to your husbands,* as is fitting in the Lord. Husbands, *love your wives,* and do not be harsh with them" (Col. 3:18–19; cf. Eph. 5:22–33; Titus 2:5; 1 Peter 3:1–7). If it were a sinful pattern for wives to be subject to their husbands' authority, Peter and Paul would not have commanded it to be maintained in Christian marriages! They do not say, for example, "Encourage thorns to grow in your garden," or "Make childbirth as painful as possible," or "Stay alienated from God, cut off from fellowship with him!" The redemption of Christ is aimed at *removing* the results of sin and of the fall in every way: "The reason the Son of God appeared was to destroy the works of the devil" (1 John 3:8). *New Testament commands concerning marriage do not perpetuate any elements of the curse or any sinful behavior patterns;* they rather reaffirm the order and distinction of roles that were there from the beginning of God's good creation.

In terms of practical application, as we grow in maturity in Christ, we will grow to delight in and rejoice in the God-ordained and wisely created differences in roles within the human family. When we understand this biblical teaching, both men and women should be able to say in their hearts, "This is what God has planned, and it is beautiful and right, and I rejoice in the way he has made me and the distinct role he has given me." There is eternal beauty and dignity and rightness in this differentiation in roles both within the Trinity and within the human family. With no sense of "better" or "worse," and with no sense of "more

---

allels in related Semitic languages to support her argument. (It is unlikely that the word means "sexual desire," for that did not begin with the fall, nor would it be part of God's curse.)

[20]See Deut. 15:6, "You shall rule over many nations, but they shall not rule over you"; Prov. 22:7, "The rich rules over the poor"; Jdg. 14:4; 15:11 (of the Philistines ruling over Israel); also Gen. 37:8; Prov. 12:24, et al.

[21]See, for example, Bilezikian, *Beyond Sex Roles,* p. 154.

[22]See Josephus, *War* 2.566, 578; 5.309; cf. the adverb in 1 Clem. 37:2; also *LSJ,* p. 1897, which defines *hypotassō* (passive)

important" or "less important," both men and women should be able to rejoice fully in the way they have been made by God.

3. Ephesians 5:21–33 and the Question of Mutual Submission. In Ephesians 5 we read:

> Wives, be subject to your husbands, as to the Lord. For the husband is the head of the wife as Christ is the head of the church, his body, and is himself its Savior. As the church is subject to Christ, so let wives also be subject in everything to their husbands. (Eph. 5:22–24)

While on the surface this would seem to confirm what we have argued above about the creation order for marriage, in recent years there has been some debate over the meaning of the verb "be subject to" (Gk. *hypotassō*) in this passage. Some people have understood it to mean "be thoughtful and considerate; act in love [toward one another]." If it is understood in this sense, then the text does not teach that a wife has any unique responsibility to submit to her husband's authority, because both husband and wife need to be considerate and loving toward one another, and because according to this view submission to an authority is not seen in this passage.[21]

However, this is not a legitimate meaning for the term *hypotassō*, which always implies a relationship of *submission to an authority*. It is used elsewhere in the New Testament of the submission of Jesus to the authority of his parents (Luke 2:51); of demons being subject to the disciples (Luke 10:17—clearly the meaning "act in love, be considerate" cannot fit here); of citizens being subject to government authorities (Rom. 13:1, 5; Titus 3:1; 1 Peter 2:13); of the universe being subject to Christ (1 Cor. 15:27; Eph. 1:22); of unseen spiritual powers being subject to Christ (1 Peter 3:22); of Christ being subject to God the Father (1 Cor. 15:28); of church members being subject to church leaders (1 Cor. 16:15–16 [see 1 Clem. 42:4]; 1 Peter 5:5); of wives being subject to their husbands (Col. 3:18; Titus 2:5; 1 Peter 3:5; cf. Eph. 5:22, 24); of the church being subject to Christ (Eph. 5:24); of servants being subject to their masters (Titus 2:9; 1 Peter 2:18); and of Christians being subject to God (Heb. 12:9; James 4:7). *None of these relationships is ever reversed;* that is, husbands are never told to be subject (*hypotassō*) to wives, nor the government to citizens, nor masters to servants, nor the disciples to demons, etc. In fact, the term is used outside the New Testament to describe the submission and obedience of soldiers in an army to those of superior rank.[22]

The primary argument that has been used in favor of taking "be subject to" in the sense "be considerate of" is the use of *hypotassō* in Ephesians 5:21. There Paul tells Christians, "Be subject *to one another.*" Several writers have argued that this means that every Christian should be subject to every other Christian, and wives and husbands especially should be "subject to one another." The phrase "mutual submission" has often been used to describe this kind of relationship, and it has been understood to imply that there is no unique kind of submission that a wife owes to her husband.

---

to mean "be obedient."

[23]Author's literal translation of Greek *idios*, "one's own."

[24]The misunderstanding of this verse has come about through an assumption that the term "one another" (*allēlous*)

However, the following context defines what Paul means by "be subject to one another" in Ephesians 5:21: he means "Be subject *to others in the church who are in positions of authority over you.*" This is explained by what follows: wives are to be subject to husbands (Eph. 5:22–24), but husbands are never told to be subject to wives. In fact, Paul tells wives to be subject "to *your own* husbands" (Eph. 5:22),[23] not to everyone in the church or to all husbands! Children are to be subject to their parents (to "obey" them, Eph. 6:1–3), but parents are never told to be subject to or to obey their children. Servants are to be subject to ("obey") their masters, but not masters to servants.[24] Therefore, the idea of mutual submission (in the sense, "everyone should be subject to everyone") is not affirmed in Ephesians 5:21.[25] Similarly, in Colossians 3:18–19 Paul says, "Wives, be subject to your husbands, as is fitting in the Lord. Husbands, love your wives, and do not be harsh with them" (see also Titus 2:4–5; 1 Peter 3:1–7).

D. Note on Application to Marriage

If our analysis is correct, then there are some practical applications, particularly within marriage, and also with regard to relationships between men and women generally.

When husbands begin to act in selfish, harsh, domineering, or even abusive and cruel ways, they should realize that this is a result of sin, a result of the fall, and is destructive and contrary to God's purposes for them. To act this way will bring great destructiveness in their lives, especially in their marriages. Husbands must rather fulfill the New Testament commands to love their wives, honor them, be considerate of them, and put them first in their interests.

Similarly, when wives feel rebellious, resentful of their husband's leadership in the family, or when they compete with their husbands for leadership in the family, they should realize that this is a result of sin, a result of the fall. They should not act that way, because to do so will bring destructive consequences to their marriages as well. A wife desiring to act in accordance with God's pattern should rather be submissive to her husband and agree that he is the leader in their home and rejoice in that.[26]

---

must be completely reciprocal (that it must mean "everyone to everyone"). Yet there are many cases where it does not take that sense, but rather means "some to others": for example, in Rev. 6:4, "so that men should slay *one another*" means "so that some would kill others"; in Gal. 6:2, "Bear *one another's* burdens" means not "Everyone should exchange burdens with everyone else," but "Some who are more able should help bear the burdens of others who are less able"; 1 Cor. 11:33, "When you come together to eat, wait for *one another*" means "those who are ready early should wait for others who are late"; etc. (cf. Luke 2:15; 21:1; 24:32). Similarly, both the following context and the meaning of *hypotassō* require that in Eph. 5:21 it means, "Those who are under authority should be subject to others among you who have authority over them."

[25]Certainly, all Christians are to love one another and to be considerate of one another. If that is what is meant by "mutual submission," then there should be no objection to it—even though that idea is not taught in Eph. 5:21, but elsewhere in the Bible, using words other than *hypotassō*. But usually the phrase "mutual submission" is used in a different sense than this, a sense that obliterates any unique authority for the husband in a marriage.

[26]See the discussion of what submission means and what it does not mean in W. Grudem, "Wives Like Sarah, and the Husbands Who Honor Them: 1 Peter 3:1–7," in *Recovering Biblical Manhood and Womanhood: A Response to Evangelical Feminism,* pp. 194–205.

Once we have said this, we must realize that there are two other, nearly opposite, distortions of the biblical pattern that can occur. If tyranny by the husband and usurpation of authority by the wife are *errors of aggressiveness,* there are two other errors, *errors of passivity* or laziness. For a husband, the other extreme from being a domineering "tyrant" is to be entirely passive and to fail to take initiative in the family—in colloquial terms, to be a "wimp." In this distortion of the biblical pattern, a husband becomes so "considerate" of his wife that he allows her to make all the decisions and even agrees when she urges him to do wrong (note this behavior in Adam, Ahab, and Solomon, among others). Often such a husband is increasingly absent (either physically or emotionally) from the home and occupies his time almost exclusively with other concerns.

The corresponding error on the part of the wife, opposite of attempting to domineer or usurp authority over her husband, is becoming entirely passive, contributing nothing to the decision-making process of the family, and being unwilling to speak words of correction to her husband, even though he is doing wrong. Submission to authority does not mean being entirely passive and agreeing with everything that the person in authority says or suggests—it is certainly not that way when we are submissive to the authority of an employer or of government officials (we can certainly differ with our government and still be subject to it), or even of the authority of the officers in a church (we can be subject to them even though we may disagree with some of their decisions). A wife can certainly be subject to the authority of her husband and still participate fully in the decision-making process of the family.

Husbands, therefore, should aim for loving, considerate, thoughtful leadership in their families. Wives should aim for active, intelligent, joyful submission to their husbands' authority. In avoiding both kinds of mistakes and following a biblical pattern, husbands and wives will discover true biblical manhood and womanhood in all of their noble dignity and joyful complementarity, as God created them to be, and will thus reflect more fully the image of God in their lives.

QUESTIONS FOR PERSONAL APPLICATION

1. If you are being honest about your feelings, do you think it is better to be a man or a woman? Are you happy with the gender God gave you or would you rather be a member of the opposite sex? How do you think God wants you to feel about that question?

2. Can you honestly say that you think members of the opposite sex are equally valuable in God's sight?

3. Before reading this chapter, have you thought of relationships in the family as reflecting something of the relationships between members of the Trinity? Do you think that is a helpful way of looking at the family? How does that make you feel about your own family relationships? Are there ways in which you might reflect God's character more fully in your own family?

4. How does the teaching of this chapter on differences in roles between men and women compare with some of the attitudes expressed in society today? If there are differences between what much of society is teaching and what Scripture teaches, do you think there will be times when it will be difficult to follow Scripture? What could your church do to help you in those situations?

5. Even apart from the questions of marriage or romantic involvement, do you think God intends us to enjoy times of fellowship with mixed groups of other Christian men and women? Why do you think God puts in our heart the desire to enjoy such fellowship? Does it also reflect something of the plurality of persons in the Trinity, together with the unity of God? Does this help you understand how it is important that unmarried people be included fully in the activities of the church? Do you think that in the past some religious groups have tended to neglect the importance of this or even wrongly to forbid such mixed fellowship among Christians? What are the dangers that should be guarded against in those situations, however?

6. If you are a husband, are you content with the role God has given you in your marriage? If you are a wife, are you content with the role God has given you in your marriage?

SPECIAL TERMS

difference in role
equality in personhood

mutual submission
primogeniture

BIBLIOGRAPHY

[Works marked * agree in general with the viewpoint presented in this chapter, while those marked ** disagree.]

Bacchiocchi, Samuele. *Women in the Church.* Berrien Springs, Mich.: Biblical Perspectives, 1987.*

Bilezikian, Gilbert. *Beyond Sex Roles: What the Bible Says About a Woman's Place in Church and Family.* 2d ed. Grand Rapids: Baker, 1985.**

Clark, Stephen B. *Man and Woman in Christ: An Examination of the Roles of Men and Women in Light of Scripture and the Social Sciences.* Ann Arbor: Servant, 1980.*

Clouse, Bonnidell, and Robert G. Clouse, eds. *Women in Ministry: Four Views.* Downers Grove, Ill.: InterVarsity Press, 1989.

Colwell, J. E. "Anthropology." In *NDT,* pp. 28–30.

Conn, H. M. "Feminist Theology." In *NDT,* pp. 255–58.

Cottrell, Jack. *Feminism and the Bible; An Introduction to Feminism for Christians.* Joplin, Mo.: College Press, 1992.*

Evans, Mary J. *Women in the Bible: An Overview of All the Crucial Passages on Women's Roles.* Downers Grove, Ill.: InterVarsity Press, 1983.**

Foh, Susan. *Women and the Word of God: A Response to Biblical Feminism.* Phillipsburg, N.J.: Presbyterian and Reformed, 1980.*

Gundry, Patricia. *Heirs Together.* Grand Rapids: Zondervan, 1980.**

_____. *Woman Be Free! The Clear Message of Scripture.* Grand Rapids: Zondervan, 1988.**

House, H. Wayne. *The Role of Women in Ministry Today.* Nashville: Thomas Nelson, 1990.*

Hurley, James. *Man and Women in Biblical Perspective.* Leicester: Inter-Varsity Press, and Grand Rapids: Zondervan, 1981.*

Jepsen, Dee. *Women: Beyond Equal Rights.* Waco, Tex.: Word, 1984.*

Jewett, Paul K. *Man as Male and Female.* Grand Rapids: Eerdmans, 1975.**

Kassian, Mary A. *Women, Creation and the Fall.* Westchester, Ill.: Crossway, 1990.**

_____. *The Feminist Gospel: The Movement to Unite Feminism With the Church.* Wheaton, Ill.: Crossway, 1992.*

Knight, George W., III. *The Role Relationship of Man and Women: New Testament Teaching.* Chicago: Moody, 1985.*

Mickelsen, Alvera, ed. *Women, Authority, and the Bible.* Downers Grove, Ill.: InterVarsity Press, 1986.**

Neuer, Werner. *Man and Woman in Christian Perspective.* Trans. by Gordon Wenham. Westchester, Ill.: Crossway, 1991.*

Piper, John. *What's the Difference? Manhood and Womanhood Defined According to the Bible.* Westchester, Ill.: Crossway, 1990.*

_____, and Wayne Grudem, eds. *Recovering Biblical Manhood and Womanhood: A Response to Evangelical Feminism.* Westchester, Ill.: Crossway, 1991.*

Spencer, Aida Besancon. *Beyond the Curse: Women Called to Ministry.* Peabody, Mass.: Hendrickson, 1985.**

Tucker, Ruth A., and Walter Liefeld. *Daughters of the Church: Women in Ministry from New Testament Times to the Present.* Grand Rapids: Zondervan, 1987.**

Van Leeuwen, Mary Stewart. *Gender and Grace: Love, Work and Parenting in a Changing World.* Leicester and Downers Grove, Ill.: InterVarsity Press, 1990.**

SCRIPTURE MEMORY PASSAGE

Colossians 3:18–19: *Wives, be subject to your husbands, as is fitting in the Lord. Husbands, love your wives, and do not be harsh with them.*

HYMN

"Blest the Man that Fears Jehovah"

This hymn is an older paraphrase of Psalm 128 set to music. It speaks about the blessings of a family that walks in God's ways. (Use the tune of "Jesus Calls Us.")

> Blest the man that fears Jehovah,
>   walking ever in his ways;
> By thy toil thou shalt be prospered

and be happy all thy days.

In thy wife thou shalt have gladness,
    She shall fill thy home with good,
Happy in her loving service
    and the joys of motherhood.

Joyful children, sons and daughters,
    shall about thy table meet,
Olive plants, in strength and beauty,
    full of hope and promise sweet.

Lo, on him that fears Jehovah
    shall this blessedness attend,
For Jehovah out of Zion
    shall to thee his blessing send.

Thou shalt see God's kingdom prosper
    all thy days, till life shall cease,
Thou shalt see thy children's children;
    on thy people, Lord, be peace.

FROM *THE PSALTER*, 1912, FROM PSALM 128

Chapter 4

THE ESSENTIAL NATURE OF MAN

What does Scripture mean by "soul" and "spirit"?
Are they the same thing?

EXPLANATION AND SCRIPTURAL BASIS

A. Introduction: Trichotomy, Dichotomy, and Monism

How many parts are there to man? Everyone agrees that we have physical bodies. Most people (both Christians and non-Christians) sense that they also have an immaterial part—a "soul" that will live on after their bodies die.

But here the agreement ends. Some people believe that in addition to "body" and "soul" we have a third part, a "spirit" that most directly relates to God. The view that man is made of three parts (*body, soul, and spirit*) is called *trichotomy*.[1] Though this has been a common view in popular evangelical Bible teaching, there are few scholarly defenses of it today. According to many trichotomists, man's *soul* includes his intellect, his emotions, and his will. They maintain that all people have such a soul, and that the different elements of the soul can either serve God or be yielded to sin. They argue that man's *spirit* is a higher faculty in man that comes alive when a person becomes a Christian (see Rom. 8:10: "If Christ is in you, although your bodies are dead because of sin, *your spirits are alive* because of righteousness"). The spirit of a person then would be that part of him or her that most directly worships and prays to God (see John 4:24; Phil. 3:3).

Others have said that "spirit" is not a separate part of man, but simply another term for "soul," and that both terms are used interchangeably in Scripture to talk about the immaterial part of man, the part that lives on after our bodies die. The view that man is made up of *two parts* (body and soul/spirit) is called *dichotomy*. Those who hold this view often

---

[1]For a defense of trichotomy, see Franz Delitzsch, *A System of Biblical Psychology,* trans. R. E. Wallis, 2d ed. (Grand Rapids: Baker, 1966).

agree that Scripture uses the word *spirit* (Heb. *rûach,* and Gk. *pneuma*) more frequently when referring to our relationship to God, but such usage (they say) is not uniform, and the word *soul* is also used in all the ways that *spirit* can be used.

Outside the realm of evangelical thought we find yet another view, the idea that man cannot exist at all apart from a physical body, and therefore there can be no separate existence for any "soul" after the body dies (although this view can allow for the resurrection of the whole person at some future time). The view that man is only one element, and that his body is the person, is called *monism*.[2] According to monism, the scriptural terms *soul* and *spirit* are just other expressions for the "person" himself, or for the person's "life." This view has not generally been adopted by evangelical theologians because so many scriptural texts seem clearly to affirm that our souls or spirits live on after our bodies die (see Gen. 35:18; Ps. 31:5; Luke 23:43, 46; Acts 7:59; Phil. 1:23–24; 2 Cor. 5:8; Heb. 12:23; and Rev. 6:9; 20:4).

But the other two views continue to be held in the Christian world today. Although dichotomy has been held more commonly through the history of the church and is far more common among evangelical scholars today, trichotomy has also had many supporters.[3]

This chapter will support the dichotomist view that man is two parts, body and soul (or spirit), but we shall also examine the arguments for trichotomy.

B. Biblical Data

Before asking whether Scripture views "soul" and "spirit" as distinct parts of man, we must at the outset make it clear that the emphasis of Scripture is on the overall unity of man as created by God. When God made man he "breathed into his nostrils the breath of life; and man became a living being" (Gen. 2:7). Here Adam is a unified person with body and soul living and acting together. This original harmonious and unified state of man will occur again when Christ returns and we are fully redeemed in our bodies as well as our souls to live with him forever (see 1 Cor. 15:51–54). Moreover, we are to grow in holiness and love for God in every aspect of our lives, in our bodies as well as in our spirits or souls (cf. 1 Cor. 7:34). We are to "cleanse ourselves from every defilement *of body and spirit,* and make holiness perfect in the fear of God" (2 Cor. 7:1).

But once we have emphasized the fact that God created us to have a unity between body and soul, and that every action we take in this life is an act of our whole person, involving to some extent both body and soul, then we can go on to point out that Scripture quite clearly teaches that there is an immaterial part of man's nature. And we can investigate what that part is like.

1. Scripture Uses "Soul" and "Spirit" Interchangeably. When we look at the usage of the biblical words translated "soul" (Heb. *nephesh* and Gk. *psychē*) and "spirit" (Heb. *rûach* and Gk. *pneuma*),[4] it appears that they are sometimes used interchangeably. For example, in

---

[2]For further information, see Millard Erickson, *Christian Theology* (Grand Rapids: Baker, 1983–85), pp. 524–27, and his notes regarding the view of J. A. T. Robinson.

[3]See Louis Berkhof, *Systematic Theology* (Grand Rapids: Eerdmans, 1939, 1941), pp. 191–92, for a survey of views held in the history of the church.

John 12:27, Jesus says, "Now is my *soul* troubled," whereas in a very similar context in the next chapter John says that Jesus was "troubled in *spirit*" (John 13:21). Similarly, we read Mary's words in Luke 1:46–47: "My *soul* magnifies the Lord, and my *spirit* rejoices in God my Savior." This seems to be quite an evident example of Hebrew parallelism, the poetic device in which the same idea is repeated using different but synonymous words. This interchangeability of terms also explains why people who have died and gone to heaven or hell can be called either "spirits" (Heb. 12:23, "the *spirits* of just men made perfect"; also 1 Peter 3:19, "*spirits* in prison") or "souls" (Rev. 6:9, "the *souls* of those who had been slain for the word of God and for the witness they had borne"; 20:4, "the *souls* of those who had been beheaded for their testimony to Jesus").

2. At Death, Scripture Says Either That the "Soul" Departs or the "Spirit" Departs. When Rachel died, Scripture says, "Her *soul* was departing (for she died)" (Gen. 35:18). Elijah prays that the dead child's "soul" would come into him again (1 Kings 17:21), and Isaiah predicts that the Servant of the Lord would "pour out his *soul* [Heb. *nephesh*] to death" (Isa. 53:12). In the New Testament God tells the rich fool, "This night your soul [Gk. *psychē*] is required of you" (Luke 12:20). On the other hand, sometimes death is viewed as the returning of the spirit to God. So David can pray, in words later quoted by Jesus on the cross, "Into your hand I commit my *spirit*" (Ps. 31:5; cf. Luke 23:46). At death, "the *spirit* returns to God who gave it" (Eccl. 12:7).[5] In the New Testament, when Jesus was dying, "he bowed his head and gave up his spirit" (John 19:30), and likewise Stephen before dying prayed, "Lord Jesus, receive my spirit" (Acts 7:59).

In response to these passages, a trichotomist might argue that they are talking about different things, for when a person dies both his soul and his spirit do in fact go to heaven. But it should be noted that Scripture nowhere says that a person's "soul and spirit" departed or went to heaven or were yielded up to God. If soul and spirit were separate and distinct things, we would expect that such language would be affirmed somewhere, if only to assure the reader that no essential part of the person is left behind. Yet we find no such language: the biblical authors do not seem to care whether they say that the soul departs or the spirit departs at death, for both seem to mean the same thing.

We should also note that these Old Testament verses quoted above indicate that it is not correct, as some have claimed, to say that the Old Testament so emphasizes the unity of

---

[4]Throughout this chapter it is important to keep in mind that several recent Bible translations (especially the NIV) do not consistently translate the Hebrew and Greek terms noted above as "soul" and "spirit," but sometimes substitute other terms such as "life," "mind," "heart," or "person." The RSV, which I quote unless another version is specified, tends to be more literal in translating these words in most cases.

In certain contexts these terms can of course be used to refer to the person's life or to the whole person, but they are also used many times to refer to a distinct part of a person's nature (see BDB, pp. 659–61, 924–25; and BAGD, pp. 674–75, 893–94, for many examples).

[5]George Ladd, *A Theology of the New Testament* (Grand Rapids: Eerdmans, 1974), says that in the Old Testament neither soul nor spirit "is conceived of as a part of man capable of surviving the death of *basar* [flesh]" (p. 459). This statement is not accurate in the light of the Old Testament verses just cited in this paragraph. Ladd's analysis in this section is heavily dependent on the work of W. D. Stacey, *The Pauline View of Man* (London: Macmillan, 1956), whom Ladd cites fourteen times on pp. 458–59. Yet Stacey himself thinks that death means extinction for human beings (Ladd, p. 463). Ladd also notes that Rudolf Bultmann vigorously denied that man has an invisible soul or spirit, but Ladd himself rejects Bultmann's view when dealing with the New Testament data (see p. 460, n. 17, and p. 464).

man that it has no conception of the existence of the soul apart from the body. Certainly several of these Old Testament passages imply that the authors recognize that a person continues to exist after his or her body dies.

3. Man Is Said to Be Either "Body and Soul" or "Body and Spirit." Jesus tells us not to fear those who "kill the body but cannot kill the soul," but that we should rather "fear him who can destroy both soul and body in hell" (Matt. 10:28). Here the word "soul" clearly must refer to the part of a person that exists after death. It cannot mean "person" or "life," for it would not make sense to speak of those who "kill the body but cannot kill the person," or who "kill the body but cannot kill the life," unless there is some aspect of the person that lives on after the body is dead. Moreover, when Jesus talks about "soul and body" he seems quite clearly to be talking about the entire person even though he does not mention "spirit" as a separate component. The word "soul" seems to stand for the entire nonphysical part of man.

On the other hand, man is sometimes said to be "body and spirit." Paul wants the Corinthian church to deliver an erring brother to Satan "for the destruction of the flesh, that his spirit may be saved in the day of the Lord Jesus" (1 Cor. 5:5). It is not that Paul has forgotten the salvation of the man's soul as well; he simply uses the word "spirit" to refer to the whole of the person's immaterial existence. Similarly, James says that "the body apart from the spirit is dead" (James 2:26), but mentions nothing about a separate soul. Moreover, when Paul speaks of growth in personal holiness, he approves the woman who is concerned with "how to be holy in body and spirit" (1 Cor. 7:34), and he suggests that this covers the whole of the person's life. Even more explicit is 2 Corinthians 7:1, where he says, "let us cleanse ourselves from every defilement of body and spirit, and make holiness perfect in the fear of God."[6] Cleansing ourselves from defilement of the "soul" or of the "spirit" covers the whole immaterial side of our existence (see also Rom. 8:10; 1 Cor. 5:3; Col. 2:5).

4. The "Soul" Can Sin or the "Spirit" Can Sin. Those who hold to trichotomy will usually agree that the "soul" can sin since they think that the soul includes the intellect, the emotions, and the will. (We see the fact that our souls can sin implied in verses such as 1 Peter 1:22; Rev. 18:14.)

The trichotomist, however, generally thinks of the "spirit" as purer than the soul, and, when renewed, as free from sin and responsive to the prompting of the Holy Spirit. This understanding (which sometimes finds its way into popular Christian preaching and writing) is not really supported by the biblical text. When Paul encourages the Corinthians to cleanse themselves "from every defilement of body and *spirit*" (2 Cor. 7:1), he clearly implies that there can be defilement (or sin) in our spirits. Similarly, he speaks of the unmarried woman who is concerned with how to be holy "in body and *spirit*" (1 Cor.

---

[6]The verse is perhaps better translated, "making holiness perfect in the view of God," since the present participle *epitelountes* suggests actions simultaneous with the main verb "cleanse," and the verse thus gives the idea that the way in which we make holiness perfect is by cleansing ourselves from every defilement of body and spirit (grammatically this would then be a modal participle).

7:34). Other verses speak in similar ways. For example, the Lord hardened the "spirit" of Sihon the king of Heshbon (Deut. 2:30). Psalm 78 speaks of the rebellious people of Israel "whose *spirit* was not faithful to God" (Ps. 78:8). A "haughty *spirit*" goes before a fall (Prov. 16:18), and it is possible for sinful people to be "proud in spirit" (Eccl. 7:8). Isaiah speaks of those "who err in spirit" (Isa. 29:24). Nebuchadnezzar's "spirit was hardened so that he dealt proudly" (Dan. 5:20). The fact that "All the ways of a man are pure in his own eyes, but the LORD weighs the spirit" (Prov. 16:2) implies that it is possible for our spirits to be wrong in God's sight. Other verses imply a possibility of sin in our spirits (see Ps. 32:2; 51:10). Finally, the fact that Scripture approves of one "who *rules his spirit*" (Prov. 16:32) implies that our spirits are not simply the spiritually pure parts of our lives that are to be followed in all cases, but that they can have sinful desires or directions as well.

5. Everything That the Soul Is Said to Do, the Spirit Is Also Said to Do, and Everything That the Spirit Is Said to Do the Soul Is Also Said to Do. Those who advocate trichotomy face a difficult problem defining clearly just what the difference is between the soul and the spirit (from their perspective). If Scripture gave clear support to the idea that our spirit is the part of us that directly relates to God in worship and prayer, while our soul includes our intellect (thinking), our emotions (feeling), and our will (deciding), then trichotomists would have a strong case. However, Scripture appears not to allow such a distinction to be made.

On the one hand, the activities of thinking, feeling, and deciding things are not said to be done by our souls only. Our spirits can also experience emotions, for example, as when Paul's "spirit was provoked within him" (Acts 17:16), or when Jesus was "troubled in spirit" (John 13:21). It is also possible to have a "downcast spirit," which is the opposite of a "cheerful heart" (Prov. 17:22).

Moreover, the functions of knowing, perceiving, and thinking are also said to be done by our spirits. For instance, Mark speaks of Jesus "perceiving [Gk. *epiginōskō*, 'knowing'] in his spirit" (Mark 2:8). When the Holy Spirit "bears witness with our spirit that we are children of God" (Rom. 8:16), our spirits receive and understand that witness, which is certainly a function of knowing something. In fact, our spirits seem to know our thoughts quite deeply, for Paul asks, "What person knows a man's thoughts except the spirit of the man which is in him?" (1 Cor. 2:11). (Cf. Isa. 29:24, speaking of those who now "err in spirit" but "will come to understanding.")

The point of these verses is not to say that it is the spirit rather than the soul that feels and thinks things, but rather that "soul" and "spirit" are both terms used of the immaterial side of people generally, and it is difficult to see any real distinction between the use of the terms.

In fact, we should not slip into the mistake of thinking that certain activities (such as thinking, feeling, or deciding things) are done by only one part of us. Rather, these activities are done by the whole person. When we think or feel things, certainly our physical bodies are involved at every point as well. Whenever we think we use the physical brain God has given us. Similarly, our brain and our entire nervous system are involved when we feel emotion, and sometimes those emotions are involved in physical sensations in other parts of our bodies. This is just to reemphasize what was said at the beginning of our discussion, that the overall focus of Scripture is primarily on man as a unity, with our physical bodies and the nonphysical part of our persons functioning together as a unity.

On the other hand, the trichotomist claim that our spirit is that element of us that relates most directly to God in worship and in prayer does not seem to be borne out by Scripture. We often read about our *soul* worshiping God and relating to him in other kinds of spiritual activity. "To you, O Lord, I lift up my *soul*" (Ps. 25:1). "For God alone my soul waits in silence" (Ps. 62:1). "Bless the Lord, O my *soul;* and all that is within me, bless his holy name!" (Ps. 103:1). "Praise the Lord, O my soul!" (Ps. 146:1). "My soul magnifies the Lord" (Luke 1:46).

These passages indicate that our souls can worship God, praise him, and give thanks to him. Our souls can pray to God, as Hannah implies when she says, "I have been pouring out my soul before the Lord" (1 Sam. 1:15). In fact, the great commandment is to "love the Lord your God with all your heart, and with all your soul, and with all your might" (Deut. 6:5; cf. Mark 12:30). Our souls can long for God and thirst for him (Ps. 42:1, 2), and can "hope in God" (Ps. 42:5). Our souls can rejoice and delight in God, for David says, "My soul shall rejoice in the Lord, exulting in his deliverance" (Ps. 35:9; cf. Isa. 61:10). The psalmist says, "My soul is consumed with longing for your ordinances at all times" (Ps. 119:20), and, "My soul keeps your testimonies; I love them exceedingly" (Ps. 119:167). There seems to be no area of life or relationship to God in which Scripture says our spirits are active rather than our souls. Both terms are used to speak of all of the aspects of our relationship to God.

However, it would be wrong, in the light of these passages, to suggest that only our souls (or spirits) worship God, for our bodies are involved in worship as well. We are a unity of body and soul/spirit. Our physical brains think about God when we worship and when we love him with all of our "minds" (Mark 12:30). David, longing to be in God's presence, can say, "My flesh faints for you, as in a dry and weary land where no water is" (Ps. 63:1). Again, we read, "My heart and flesh sing for joy to the living God" (Ps. 84:2). It is obvious that when we pray aloud or sing praise to God, our lips and our vocal cords are involved, and sometimes worship and prayer in Scripture involves clapping of hands (Ps. 47:1) or lifting of hands to God (Pss. 28:2; 63:4; 134:2; 143:6; 1 Tim. 2:8). Moreover, the playing of musical instruments in praise to God is an act that involves our physical bodies as well as the physical materials of which the musical instruments are made (see Ps. 150:3–5). We worship him as whole persons.

In conclusion, Scripture does not seem to support any distinction between soul and spirit. There does not seem to be a satisfactory answer to the questions that we may address to a trichotomist, "What can the spirit do that the soul cannot do? What can the soul do that the spirit cannot do?"

C. Arguments for Trichotomy

Those who adopt the trichotomist position have appealed to a number of Scripture passages in support of it. We list here the ones that are most commonly used.

1. 1 Thessalonians 5:23. "May the God of peace himself sanctify you wholly; and may your *spirit and soul and body* be kept sound and blameless at the coming of our Lord Jesus Christ" (1 Thess. 5:23). Does not this verse clearly speak of three parts to man?

2. Hebrews 4:12. "The word of God is living and active, sharper than any two-edged sword, piercing to the *division of soul and spirit,* of joints and marrow, and discerning the thoughts and intentions of the heart" (Heb. 4:12). If the sword of Scripture divides soul and spirit, then are these not two separate parts of man?

3. 1 Corinthians 2:14–3:4. This passage speaks of different kinds of people, those who are "of the flesh" (Gk. *sarkinos,* 1 Cor. 3:1); those who are "unspiritual" (Gk. *psychikos,* lit. "soul-ish," 1 Cor. 2:14); and those who are "spiritual" (Gk. *pneumatikos,* 1 Cor. 2:15). Do not these categories suggest that there are different sorts of people, the non-Christians who are "of the flesh," "unspiritual" Christians who follow the desires of their souls, and more mature Christians who follow the desires of their spirits? Would this not suggest that soul and spirit are different elements of our nature?

4. 1 Corinthians 14:14. When Paul says, "If I pray in a tongue, my spirit prays but my mind is unfruitful" (1 Cor. 14:14), is he not implying that his mind does something different from his spirit, and would not this support the trichotomist's argument that our mind and our thinking are to be assigned to our souls, not to our spirit?

5. The Argument From Personal Experience. Many trichotomists say that they have a spiritual perception, a spiritual awareness of God's presence which affects them in a way that they know to be different from their ordinary thinking processes and different from their emotional experiences. They ask, "If I do not have a spirit that is distinct from my thoughts and my emotions, then what exactly is it that I feel that is different from my thoughts and my emotions, something that I can only describe as worshiping God in my spirit and sensing his presence in my spirit? Isn't there something in me that is more than just my intellect and my emotions and my will, and shouldn't this be called my spirit?"

6. Our Spirit Is What Makes Us Different From Animals. Some trichotomists argue that both humans and animals have souls, but maintain that it is the presence of a spirit that makes us different from animals.

7. Our Spirit Is What Comes Alive at Regeneration. Trichotomists also argue that when we become Christians our spirits come alive: "But if Christ is in you, although your bodies are dead because of sin, your spirits are alive because of righteousness" (Rom. 8:10).

Now we can consider the seven points given above:

D. Responses to Arguments for Trichotomy

1. 1 Thessalonians 5:23. The phrase "your spirit and soul and body" is by itself inconclusive. Paul could be simply piling up synonyms for emphasis, as is sometimes done elsewhere in Scripture. For example, Jesus says, "You shall love the Lord your God with all your *heart,* and with all your *soul,* and with all your *mind*" (Matt. 22:37). Does this mean that the soul is different from the mind or from the heart?[7] The problem is even greater in Mark 12:30: "You shall love the Lord your God with all your *heart,* and with all your *soul,* and with all your *mind,* and with all your *strength.*" If we go on the principle that such lists of terms tell us about more parts to man, then if we also add spirit to this list (and perhaps body as well), we would have five or six parts to man! But that is certainly a false conclusion. It is far better to understand Jesus as simply piling up roughly synonymous terms for emphasis to demonstrate that we must love God with all of our being.

Likewise, in 1 Thessalonians 5:23 Paul is not saying that soul and spirit are distinct entities, but simply that, whatever our immaterial part is called, he wants God to continue to sanctify us wholly to the day of Christ.

2. Hebrews 4:12. This verse, which talks about the Word of God "piercing to the division of soul and spirit, of joints and marrow," is best understood in a way similar to 1 Thessalonians 5:23. The author is not saying that the Word of God can divide "soul *from* spirit," but he is using a number of terms (soul, spirit, joints, marrow, thoughts and intentions of the heart) that speak of the deep inward parts of our being that are not hidden from the penetrating power of the Word of God. If we wish to call these our "soul," then Scripture pierces into the midst of it and divides it and discovers its inmost intentions. If we wish to call this inmost nonphysical side of our being our "spirit," then Scripture penetrates into the midst of it and divides it and knows its deepest intentions and thoughts. Or if we wish to think metaphorically of our inmost being as hidden in our joints and in the marrow, then we can think of Scripture being like a sword that divides our joints or that pierces deeply into our bones and even divides the marrow in the midst of the bones.[8] In all of these cases the Word of God is so powerful that it will search out and expose all disobedience and lack of submission to God. In any case, soul and spirit are not thought of as separate parts; they are simply additional terms for our inmost being.

3. 1 Corinthians 2:14–3:4. Paul certainly distinguishes a person who is "natural" (*psychikos,* "soul-ish") from one that is "spiritual" (*pneumatikos,* "spiritual") in 1 Corinthians 2:14–3:4. But in this context "spiritual" seems to mean "influenced by the Holy Spirit," since the entire passage is talking about the work of the Holy Spirit in revealing truth to believers. In this context, "spiritual" might almost be translated "Spiritual." But the passage does not imply that Christians have a spirit whereas non-Christians do not, or that the spirit of a Christian is alive while the spirit of a non-Christian is not. Paul is not talking about different parts of man at all, but about coming under the influence of the Holy Spirit.

4. 1 Corinthians 14:14. When Paul says, "My *spirit* prays but my mind is unfruitful," he means he does not understand the content of what he is praying. He does imply that there is a nonphysical component to his being, a "spirit" within him that can pray to God. But

---

[7] The "heart" in Scripture is an expression for the deepest, inmost thoughts and feelings of a person (see Gen. 6:5, 6; Lev. 19:17; Pss. 14:1; 15:2; 37:4; 119:10; Prov. 3:5; Acts 2:37; Rom. 2:5; 10:9; 1 Cor. 4:5; 14:25; Heb. 4:12; 1 Peter 3:4; Rev. 2:23, et al.).

[8] Note that we do not divide joints from marrow, for joints are the places where bones meet, not the places where joints meet marrow.

nothing in this verse suggests that he regards his spirit as different from his soul. Such a misunderstanding results only if it is assumed that "mind" is part of the soul—a trichotomist claim that, as we noted above, is very difficult to substantiate from Scripture. Paul probably could equally have said, "My soul prays but my mind is unfruitful."[9] The point is simply that there is a nonphysical element to our existence that can at times function apart from our conscious awareness of how it is functioning.

5. The Argument From Personal Experience. Christians have a "spiritual perception," an inner awareness of the presence of God experienced in worship and in prayer. At this deep inward level we can also at times feel spiritually troubled, or depressed, or perhaps have a sense of the presence of hostile demonic forces. Often this perception is distinct from our conscious, rational thought processes. Paul realizes that at times his spirit prays but his mind does not understand (1 Cor. 14:14). But does inward spiritual perception occur in something other than what the Bible calls our "soul"? If we were using the vocabulary of Mary, we would be happy to say, "My soul magnifies the Lord" (Luke 1:46). David would say, "Bless the Lord, O my soul" (Ps. 103:1). Jesus would tell us to love God with all our soul (Mark 12:30). The apostle Paul uses the word *spirit,* but it is simply a difference in terminology and does not point to a different part of man. There is a "spirit" within us that can perceive things in the spiritual realm (note Rom. 8:16; also Acts 17:16), but we could just as well speak of it as our "soul" and mean the same thing, for Scripture uses both terms.

6. What Makes Us Different From Animals? It is true that we have spiritual abilities that make us different from animals:[10] we are able to relate to God in worship and prayer, and we enjoy spiritual life in fellowship with God who is spirit. But we should not assume that we have a distinct element called "spirit" that allows us to do this, for with our minds we can love God, read and understand his words, and believe his Word to be true. Our souls can worship God and rejoice in him (see above). Our bodies will also be resurrected and live with God forever. Therefore we do not have to say that we have a part distinct from our souls and bodies that makes us different from animals, for our souls and bodies (including our minds) relate to God in ways animals never can. Rather, what makes us different from animals is the spiritual abilities that God has given to both our bodies and souls (or spirits).

The question of whether an animal has a "soul" simply depends on how we define soul. If we define "soul" to mean "the intellect, emotions, and will," then we will have to conclude that at least the higher animals have a soul. But if we define our "soul" as we have in this chapter, to mean the immaterial element of our nature that relates to God (Ps. 103:1; Luke 1:46, et al.) and lives forever (Rev. 6:9), then animals do not have a soul. The fact that the Hebrew word *nephesh,* "soul," is sometimes used of animals (Gen. 1:21; 9:4) shows that

---

[9]However, it is much more characteristic of Paul's terminology to use the word "spirit" to talk about our relationship to God in worship and in prayer. Paul does not use the word "soul" (Gk. *psychē*) very frequently (14 times, compared with 101 occurrences in the New Testament as a whole), and when he does, he often uses it simply to refer to a person's "life," or as a synonym for a person himself, as in Rom. 9:3; 13:1; 16:4; Phil. 2:30. Use of the word "soul" to refer to the non-physical side of man is more characteristic of the gospels, and of many passages in the Old Testament.

[10]See chapter 2, pp. 40–44, on the numerous differences between human beings and animals.

the word can sometimes simply mean "life"; it does not mean that animals have the same kind of soul as man.[11]

7. Does Our Spirit Come Alive at Regeneration? The human spirit is not something that is dead in an unbeliever but comes to life when someone trusts in Christ, because the Bible talks about unbelievers having a spirit that is obviously alive but is in rebellion against God—whether Sihon, King of Heshbon (Deut. 2:30: the Lord "hardened his spirit"), or Nebuchadnezzar (Dan. 5:20: "his spirit was hardened so that he dealt proudly"), or the unfaithful people of Israel (Ps. 78:8: their "spirit was not faithful to God"). When Paul says, "Your spirits are alive because of righteousness" (Rom. 8:10), he apparently means "alive to God," but he does not imply that our spirits were completely "dead" before, only that they were living out of fellowship with God and were dead in that sense.[12] In the same way, we as whole persons were "dead" in "trespasses and sins" (Eph. 2:1), but we were made alive to God, and we now must consider ourselves "dead to sin and alive to God" (Rom. 6:11). It is not just that one part of us (called the spirit) has been made alive; we as whole persons are a "new creation" in Christ (2 Cor. 5:17).

8. Conclusion. Although the arguments for trichotomy do have some force, none of them provides conclusive evidence that would overcome the wide testimony of Scripture showing that the terms *soul* and *spirit* are frequently interchangeable and are in many cases synonymous.

We might also note the observation of Louis Berkhof on the origin of trichotomy:

> The tripartite conception of man originated in Greek philosophy, which conceived of the relation of the body and the spirit of man to each other after the analogy of the mutual relation between the material universe and God. It was thought that, just as the latter could enter into communion with each other only by means of a third substance or an intermediate being, so the former could enter into mutual vital relationships only by means of a third or intermediate element, namely, the soul.[13]

Some trichotomists today have a tendency to adopt a related error that also was found in Greek philosophy—the idea that the material world, including our bodies, is essentially evil and something to be escaped from. The danger is to say that the realm of the "spirit" is the only thing that is really important, with a resultant depreciation of the value of our physical bodies as created by God and "very good" (Gen. 1:31), and therefore as something to be presented to God in service for him (Rom. 12:1).

---

[11]In fact, one passage even speculates about "the spirit of the beast" in contrast with "the spirit of man," (Eccl. 3:21), but the context (vv. 18–22) is one expressing a worldly, cynical perspective that shows the vanity of life and argues that man is but a beast (v. 18): in the overall context of the book it is not clear that this is something the author is encouraging his readers to believe.

[12]Another common view of Rom. 8:10 is that Paul is not referring to our human spirits at all but that *pneuma* here means the Holy Spirit, as in vv. 9 and 11, so that the phrase means, "The Spirit is life [for you] because of righteousness": see Douglas Moo, Romans 1–8, *Wycliffe Exegetical Commentary* (Chicago: Moody, 1991), p. 525; John Murray, *The Epistle to the Romans*, NIC, 2 vols. (Grand Rapids: Eerdmans, 1959, 1965), 1:289–91.

[13]Berkhof, *Systematic Theology*, p. 191.

Trichotomy can also have an anti-intellectual tendency. If we think of the spirit as that element of us that relates most directly to God, and if we think that the spirit is something distinct from our intellect, emotions, and will, we can easily fall into an anti-intellectual kind of Christianity that thinks that vigorous academic work is somehow "unspiritual"—a view that contradicts Jesus' command to love God with all our "mind" (Mark 12:30) and Paul's desire to "take every thought captive to obey Christ" (2 Cor. 10:5). Such a separation of the realm of the "spirit" from the realm of the intellect can too easily lead to a neglect of sound doctrine or of the need for extensive teaching and knowledge of the Word of God—in contradiction to Paul's goal that he would work among God's people to further both their "faith" and their "knowledge of the truth which accords with godliness" (Titus 1:1; cf. v. 9). Similarly, if we think of our spirits as a distinct part of us that relates most directly to God, we can easily begin to neglect the role of Bible study and mature wisdom in making decisions, and place too much reliance on "spiritual" discernment in the realm of guidance, an emphasis that has, through the history of the church, led many zealous Christians astray into false teaching and unwise practices. Finally, trichotomy can subtly influence us to think that our emotions are not important or not really spiritual, since they are thought to be part of our soul, not part of our spirit.

By contrast, if we hold to a view of dichotomy that upholds the overall unity of man, it will be much easier to avoid the error of depreciating the value of our intellects, emotions, or physical bodies. We will not think of our bodies as inherently evil or unimportant. Such a view of dichotomy within unity will also help us to remember that, in this life, there is a continual interaction between our body and our spirit, and that they affect each other: "A cheerful heart is good medicine, but a downcast spirit dries up the bones" (Prov. 17:22).[14]

Moreover, a healthy emphasis on dichotomy within an overall unity reminds us that Christian growth must include all aspects of our lives. We are continually to "cleanse ourselves from every defilement of body and spirit, and make holiness perfect in the fear of God" (2 Cor. 7:1). We are to be "increasing in the knowledge of God" (Col. 1:10), and our emotions and desires are to conform increasingly to the "desires of the Spirit" (Gal. 5:17), including an increase in godly emotions such as peace, joy, love,[15] and so forth (Gal. 5:22).

E. Scripture Does Speak of an Immaterial Part of Man That Can Exist Without His Body

A number of non-Christian philosophers have vigorously challenged the idea that man has any immaterial part at all such as a soul or spirit.[16] Perhaps partially in response to such criticism, some evangelical theologians have seemed hesitant to affirm dichotomy in human existence.[17] They have instead affirmed repeatedly that the Bible views man as a unity—a

---

[14]Although many passages of Scripture remind us that our bodies and our spirits do interact with each other and affect one another, Scripture does not tell us very much about how they interact. Berkhof wisely says, "Body and soul are distinct substances, which do interact, though their mode of interaction escapes human scrutiny and remains a mystery for us" (*Systematic Theology*, p. 195).

[15]Some people will object that love is not merely an emotion, because it shows itself in actions and often we can will to perform loving actions toward others even when we do not feel love toward them. I agree with this, but there certainly is an emotional component to love—we can feel love toward others—and we would lose much of the richness of our relationship to God and others if we tried to deny this.

fact which is true but should not be used to deny that Scripture also views man's unified nature as made up of two distinct elements. Of course, philosophers who assume that there is no spiritual realm beyond the reach of our sense perception, and who then go from that assumption to argue on the basis of our sense perception that there is no God, or heaven, or angels, or demons, will use similar arguments to deny the existence of a distinct soul within human beings. The perception that we have a spirit or soul belongs to the invisible, spiritual realm, and is, even in Christians, generally only a faint, subjective perception. Therefore, our knowledge of the existence of the human soul must be primarily based on Scripture, in which God clearly testifies to the existence of this immaterial aspect of our beings. The fact that this truth about our existence cannot be clearly known apart from the testimony of Scripture should not cause us to shrink from affirming it.

Scripture is very clear that we do have a soul that is distinct from our physical bodies, which not only can function somewhat independently of our ordinary thought processes (1 Cor. 14:14; Rom. 8:16), but also, when we die, is able to go on consciously acting and relating to God apart from our physical bodies. Jesus told the dying thief, "Today you will be with me in Paradise" (Luke 23:43), even though, for both of them, their physical bodies were soon to die. When Stephen was dying, he knew he would immediately pass into the presence of the Lord, for he prayed, "Lord Jesus, receive my *spirit*" (Acts 7:59). Paul does not fear death, for he says, "My desire is to depart and be with Christ, for that is far better" (Phil. 1:23). He contrasts that with remaining in this life, which he calls "to remain in the flesh" (Phil. 1:24). In fact, he says, "We would rather be *away from the body* and at home with the Lord" (2 Cor. 5:8), indicating a confidence that if he were to die physically his spirit would go into the Lord's presence and there enjoy fellowship with the Lord at once. The book of Revelation reminds us that "the *souls* of those who had been slain for the word of God and for the witness they had borne" (Rev. 6:9) are in heaven and are able to cry out to God to bring justice on the earth (Rev. 6:10; cf. also 20:4).

Therefore, although we must agree that, in this life, Scripture views us as a unity in which body and spirit act together as one person, nonetheless, there will be a time between our death and the day Christ returns when our spirits will temporarily exist apart from our physical bodies.

F. Where Do Our Souls Come From?

What is the origin of our individual souls? Two views have been common in the history of the church.

Creationism is the view that God creates a new soul for each person and sends it to that person's body sometime between conception and birth. *Traducianism,* on the other hand, holds that the soul as well as the body of a child are inherited from the baby's mother and father at the time of conception. Both views have had numerous defenders in the history of the church, with creationism eventually becoming the prevailing view in the Roman Catholic Church. Luther was in favor of traducianism, while Calvin favored creationism.

---

[16]See the discussion in Millard Erickson, *Christian Theology,* pp. 530–36, with notes to some literature.

[17]See, for example, G. C. Berkouwer, *Man, the Image of God* (Grand Rapids: Eerdmans, 1962), pp. 194–233.

On the other hand, there are some later Calvinist theologians such as A. H. Strong who favored traducianism (as do most Lutherans today). Creationism has had many modern evangelical advocates as well.[18]

There is one other popular view called *pre-existentianism,* namely, that the souls of people exist in heaven long before their bodies are conceived in the wombs of their mothers, and that God then brings the soul to earth to be joined with the baby's body as he or she grows in the womb. But this view is not held by either Roman Catholic or Protestant theologians and is dangerously akin to ideas of reincarnation found in Eastern religions. Moreover, there is no support for this view in Scripture. Before we were conceived in the wombs of our mothers, we simply did not exist. We were not. Of course, God looked forward into the future and knew that we would exist, but that is far removed from saying that we actually did exist at some previous time. Such an idea would tend to make us view this present life as transitional or unimportant and make us think of life in the body as less desirable and the bearing and raising of children as less important.

In favor of traducianism it may be argued that God created man in his own image (Gen. 1:27), and this includes a likeness to God in the amazing ability to "create" other human beings like ourselves. Therefore, just as the rest of the animal and plant world bears descendants "according to their kinds" (Gen. 1:24), so Adam and Eve also were able to bear children who were like themselves, with a spiritual nature as well as a physical body. This would imply that the spirits or souls of Adam and Eve's children were derived from Adam and Eve themselves. Moreover, Scripture sometimes can speak of descendants being somehow present in the body of someone in the previous generation, as when the author of Hebrews says that when Melchizedek met Abraham, "Levi . . . was still in the loins of his ancestor" (Heb. 7:10). Finally, traducianism could explain how the sins of the parents can be passed on to the children without making God directly responsible for the creation of a soul that is sinful or has a disposition that would tend toward sin.

However, the biblical arguments in favor of creationism seem to speak more directly to the issue and give quite strong support for this view. First, Psalm 127 says that "sons are a heritage from the LORD, the fruit of the womb a reward" (Ps. 127:3). This indicates that not only the soul, but also the entire person of the child, including his or her body, is a gift from God. From this standpoint, it seems strange to think of the mother and father as being responsible by themselves for any aspect of the child's existence. Was it not the Lord who, David says, "knit me together in my mother's womb" (Ps. 139:13)? Isaiah says that God gives breath to the people on the earth and "spirit to those who walk in it" (Isa. 42:5).[19] Zechariah talks of God as the one "who forms the spirit of man within him" (Zech. 12:1 NIV). The author of Hebrews speaks of God as "the Father of spirits" (Heb. 12:9). It is hard to escape the conclusion from these passages that God is the one who creates our spirits or souls.

Yet we must be cautious in drawing conclusions from this data. God usually acts through secondary causes. God often brings about the results he seeks through the actions of human beings. Certainly this is so in the conception and bearing of children. Even if we say that

---

[18]See, for example, Berkhof, *Systematic Theology,* pp. 196–201.

God does create individual souls for human beings before they are born, and that he is the one who allows children to be conceived and born, we must also recognize that apart from the physical union of man and woman in the conception of a child, no children are born! So we must not make the mistake of saying that the father and mother have no role in the creation of the child. Even if we say that God is the "Father of spirits" and the Creator of every human soul, just as he is the Maker and Creator of each of us, we must still also affirm that God carries out this creative activity through the amazing process of human procreation. Whether God involves the human mother and father to some degree in the process of the creation of a soul as well as of a physical body, is impossible for us to say. It is something that occurs in the invisible realm of the spirit, which we do not have information about except from Scripture. And on this point Scripture simply does not give us enough information to decide.

However, the arguments listed above in favor of traducianism must be said not to be very compelling ones. The fact that Adam and Eve bear children in their own image (see Gen. 5:3) could suggest that children somehow inherit a soul from their parents, but it might also indicate that God gives an individually created soul to the child and that that soul is consistent with the hereditary traits and personality characteristics that God allowed the child to have through its descent from its parents. The idea that Levi was still in the body of Abraham (Heb. 7:10) is best understood in a representative, or figurative, sense, not in a literal sense. Moreover, it is not simply Levi's soul that is talked about in any case, but Levi himself, as a whole person, including body and soul—yet Levi's body was certainly not physically present in any meaningful sense in Abraham's body, for there was no distinct combination of genes at that time that could be said to be Levi and no one else. Finally, since God brings about events in the physical world that are consistent with the voluntary activities of human beings, there does not seem to be any real theological difficulty in saying that God gives each child a human soul that has tendencies to sin that are similar to the tendencies found in the parents. In fact, we read in the Ten Commandments of God "visiting the iniquity of the fathers upon the children to the third and the fourth generation of those who hate [him]" (Ex. 20:5), and, quite apart from the question of the human soul, we know from human experience that children do in fact tend to imitate both the good and bad traits in their parents' lives, not only as a result of imitation but also because of hereditary disposition. For God to give each child a human soul that accords with the imitation of parents that we see in the lives of children would simply be an indication that God, in creating a human soul, acts consistently with the way he acts in relation to the human race in other matters as well.

In conclusion, it seems hard to avoid the testimony of Scripture to the effect that God actively creates each human soul, just as he is active in all the events of his creation. But the degree to which he allows the use of intermediate or secondary causes (that is, inheritance from parents) is simply not explained for us in Scripture. Therefore, it does not seem profitable for us to spend any more time speculating on this question.

---

[19]Instead of "spirit" the NIV translates "life," but the word is *rûach,* the common Hebrew word for "spirit."

CHAPTER 4 · THE ESSENTIAL NATURE OF MAN

QUESTIONS FOR PERSONAL APPLICATION

1. In your own Christian experience, are you aware that you are more than just a physical body, that you have a nonphysical part that might be called a soul or spirit? At what times do you especially become aware of the existence of your spirit? Can you describe what it is like to know the witness of the Holy Spirit with your spirit that you are God's child (Rom. 8:16), or to have in your spirit a consciousness of God's presence (John 4:23; Phil. 3:3), or to be troubled in your spirit (John 12:27; 13:21; Acts 17:16; 2 Cor. 2:13), or to have your spirit worship God (Luke 1:47; Ps. 103:1), or to love God with all your soul (Mark 12:30)? By contrast, are there times when you feel spiritually dull or insensitive? Do you think that one aspect of Christian growth might include an increasing sensitivity to the state of your soul or spirit?

2. Before reading this chapter, did you hold to dichotomy or trichotomy? Now what is your view? If you have changed to an acceptance of dichotomy after reading this chapter, do you think you will have a higher appreciation for the activities of your body, your mind, and your emotions? If you hold to trichotomy, how can you guard against some of the dangers mentioned in this chapter?

3. When you are praying or singing praise to God, is it enough simply to sing or speak words, without being aware of what you are saying? Is it enough to be aware of what you are saying without really meaning it? If you really mean the words with your whole being, then what aspects of your person would be involved in genuine prayer and worship? Do you think you tend to neglect one or another aspect at times?

4. Since Scripture encourages us to grow in holiness in our bodies as well as our spirits (2 Cor. 7:1), what specifically would it mean for you to be more obedient to that command?

SPECIAL TERMS

creationism
dichotomy
monism
soul

spirit
traducianism
trichotomy

BIBLIOGRAPHY

Note: Several of the books listed in the bibliography for chapter 2, on the creation of man in the image of God, also have sections on the essential nature of man and the origin of the soul.

Colwell, J. E. "Anthropology." In *NDT,* pp. 28–30.

Cooper, John W. *Body, Soul, and Life Everlasting: Biblical Anthropology and the Monism-Dualism Debate.* Grand Rapids: Eerdmans, 1989.

Delitzsch, F. *A System of Biblical Psychology.* Trans. by R. E. Wallis. 2d ed. Grand Rapids: Baker, 1966.

Gundry, Robert H. *Sōma in Biblical Theology With Emphasis on Pauline Anthropology.* Grand Rapids: Zondervan, 1987.

Heard, J. B. *The Tripartite Nature of Man.* 5th ed. Edinburgh: T. & T. Clark, 1882.

Hoekema, Anthony A. "The Whole Person." In *Created in God's Image.* Grand Rapids: Eerdmans, and Exeter: Paternoster, 1986, pp. 203–26.

Ladd, George Eldon. "The Pauline Psychology." In *A Theology of the New Testament.* Grand Rapids: Eerdmans, 1974, pp. 457–78.

Laidlaw, John. *The Bible Doctrine of Man.* 2d ed. Edinburgh: T. & T. Clark, 1905.

McDonald, H. D. "Man, Doctrine of." In *EDT,* pp. 676–80.

SCRIPTURE MEMORY PASSAGE

2 Corinthians 7:1: *Since we have these promises, beloved, let us cleanse ourselves from every defilement of body and spirit, and make holiness perfect in the fear of God.*

HYMN

"Be Still, My Soul"

>Be still, my soul: the Lord is on thy side;
>>Bear patiently the cross of grief or pain;
>
>Leave to thy God to order and provide;
>>In ev'ry change he faithful will remain.
>
>Be still, my soul: thy best, thy heav'nly friend
>>Through thorny ways leads to a joyful end.
>
>Be still, my soul: thy God doth undertake
>>To guide the future as he has the past.
>
>Thy hope, thy confidence let nothing shake;
>>All now mysterious shall be bright at last.
>
>Be still, my soul: the waves and winds still know
>>His voice who ruled them while he dwelt below.
>
>Be still, my soul: when dearest friends depart,
>>And all is darkened in the vale of tears,
>
>Then shalt thou better know his love, his heart,
>>Who comes to soothe thy sorrow and thy fears.
>
>Be still, my soul: thy Jesus can repay
>>From his own fullness all he takes away.
>
>Be still, my soul: the hour is hast'ning on

When we shall be forever with the Lord,
When disappointment, grief, and fear are gone,
   Sorrow forgot, love's purest joys restored.
Be still, my soul: when change and tears are past,
   All safe and blessed we shall meet at last.

AUTHOR: KATHARINA VON SCHLEGEL, BORN 1697

Chapter 5

SIN

What is sin? Where did it come from?
Do we inherit a sinful nature from Adam?
Do we inherit guilt from Adam?

EXPLANATION AND SCRIPTURAL BASIS

A. The Definition of Sin

The history of the human race as presented in Scripture is primarily a history of man in a state of sin and rebellion against God and of God's plan of redemption to bring man back to himself. Therefore, it is appropriate now to consider the nature of the sin that separates man from God.

We may define sin as follows: *Sin is any failure to conform to the moral law of God in act, attitude, or nature.* Sin is here defined in relation to God and his moral law. Sin includes not only individual *acts* such as stealing or lying or committing murder, but also *attitudes* that are contrary to the attitudes God requires of us. We see this already in the Ten Commandments, which not only prohibit sinful actions but also wrong attitudes: "You shall not covet your neighbor's house. You shall not covet your neighbor's wife, or his manservant or maidservant, his ox or donkey, or anything that belongs to your neighbor" (Ex. 20:17 NIV). Here God specifies that a desire to steal or to commit adultery is also sin in his sight. The Sermon on the Mount also prohibits sinful attitudes such as anger (Matt. 5:22) or lust (Matt. 5:28). Paul lists attitudes such as jealousy, anger, and selfishness (Gal. 5:20) as things that are works of the flesh opposed to the desires of the Spirit (Gal. 5:20). Therefore a life that is pleasing to God is one that has moral purity not only in its actions, but also in its desires of heart. In fact, the greatest commandment of all requires that our heart be filled with an attitude of love for God: "You shall love the Lord your God with all your heart, and with all your soul, and with all your mind, and with all your strength" (Mark 12:30).

The definition of sin given above specifies that sin is a failure to conform to God's moral law not only in *action* and in *attitude,* but also in our *moral nature.* Our very nature, the internal character that is the essence of who we are as persons, can also be sinful. Before we were redeemed by Christ, not only did we do sinful acts and have sinful attitudes, we were also sinners by nature. So Paul can say that "while *we were yet sinners* Christ died for us" (Rom. 5:8), or that previously "we were *by nature* children of wrath, like the rest of mankind" (Eph. 2:3). Even while asleep, an unbeliever, though not committing sinful actions or actively nurturing sinful attitudes, is still a "sinner" in God's sight; he or she still has a sinful nature that does not conform to God's moral law.

Other definitions of the essential character of sin have been suggested. Probably the most common definition is to say that the essence of sin is selfishness.[1] However, such a definition is unsatisfactory because (1) Scripture itself does not define sin this way. (2) Much self-interest is good and approved by Scripture, as when Jesus commands us to "lay up for yourselves treasures in heaven" (Matt. 6:20), or when we seek to grow in sanctification and Christian maturity (1 Thess. 4:3), or even when we come to God through Christ for salvation. God certainly appeals to the self-interest of sinful people when he says, "Turn back, turn back from your evil ways; for why will you die, O house of Israel?" (Ezek. 33:11). To define the essential character of sin as selfishness will lead many people to think that they should abandon all desire for their own personal benefit, which is certainly contrary to Scripture.[2] (3) Much sin is not selfishness in the ordinary sense of the term—people can show *selfless* devotion to a false religion or to secular and humanistic educational or political goals that are contrary to Scripture, yet these would not be due to "selfishness" in any ordinary sense of the word. Moreover, hatred of God, idolatry, and unbelief are not generally due to selfishness, but they are very serious sins. (4) Such a definition could suggest that there was wrongdoing or sinfulness even on God's part, since God's highest goal is to seek his own glory (Isa. 42:8; 43:7, 21; Eph. 1:12). But such a conclusion is clearly wrong.

It is far better to define sin in the way Scripture does, in relationship to God's law and his moral character. John tells us that "sin is lawlessness" (1 John 3:4). When Paul seeks to demonstrate the universal sinfulness of mankind, he appeals to the law of God, whether the written law given to the Jew (Rom. 2:17–29) or the unwritten law that operates in the consciences of Gentiles who, by their behavior, "show that what the law requires is written

---

[1]See, for example, A. H. Strong, *Systematic Theology* (Valley Forge, Pa.: Judson, 1907), pp. 567–73. However, Strong defines selfishness in a very specific way that is different from the ordinary sense of the term when used to mean simply self-interest or self-interest at the expense of other persons. Strong regards selfishness as "that choice of self as the supreme end which constitutes the antithesis of supreme love to God" (p. 567) and as "a fundamental and positive choice of preference of self instead of God, as the object of affection and the supreme end of being" (p. 572). By thus defining selfishness in relationship to God, and specifically as the opposite of love for God, and as the opposite of "love for that which is most characteristic and fundamental in God, namely, his holiness" (p. 567), Strong has actually made "selfishness" approximately equivalent to our definition (lack of conformity to the moral law of God), especially in the area of attitude (which, he explains, results in actions). When Strong defines "selfishness" in this unusual way, his definition is not really inconsistent with Scripture, for he is just saying that sin is the opposite of the great commandment to love God with all our heart. The problem with this definition, however, is that he uses the word *selfishness* in a way in which it is not commonly understood in English, and therefore his definition of sin is frequently open to misunderstanding. Our discussion in this section is not objecting to sin as selfishness in the unusual sense given by Strong, but rather in the way in which the term *selfishness* is ordinarily understood.

[2]Of course, selfishness that seeks our own good at the expense of others is wrong, and that is what is meant when Scripture tells us to "do nothing from selfishness or empty conceit, but with humility of mind let each of you regard one another as more important than himself" (Phil. 2:3 NASB). Yet the distinction between selfishness in the wrong sense and scripturally enlightened self-interest is unclear in the minds of many people.

on their hearts" (Rom. 2:15). In each case their sinfulness is demonstrated by their lack of conformity to the moral law of God.

Finally, we should note that this definition emphasizes the seriousness of sin. We realize from experience that sin is harmful to our lives, that it brings pain and destructive consequences to us and to others affected by it. But to define sin as failure to conform to the moral law of God, is to say that sin is more than simply painful and destructive—it is also *wrong* in the deepest sense of the word. In a universe created by God, *sin ought not to be approved*. Sin is directly opposite to all that is good in the character of God, and just as God necessarily and eternally delights in himself and in all that he is, so God necessarily and eternally hates sin. It is, in essence, the contradiction of the excellence of his moral character. It contradicts his holiness, and he must hate it.

B. The Origin of Sin

Where did sin come from? How did it come into the universe? First, we must clearly affirm that God himself did not sin, and God is not to be blamed for sin. It was man who sinned, and it was angels who sinned, and in both cases they did so by willful, voluntary choice. To blame God for sin would be blasphemy against the character of God. "His work is perfect; for all his ways are justice. A God of faithfulness and without iniquity, just and right is he" (Deut. 32:4). Abraham asks with truth and force in his words, "Shall not the Judge of all the earth do right?" (Gen. 18:25). And Elihu rightly says, "Far be it from God that he should do wickedness, and from the Almighty that he should do wrong" (Job 34:10). In fact, it is impossible for God even to desire to do wrong: "God cannot be tempted with evil and he himself tempts no one" (James 1:13).

Yet, on the other hand, we must guard against an opposite error: it would be wrong for us to say there is an eternally existing evil power in the universe similar to or equal to God himself in power. To say this would be to affirm what is called an ultimate "dualism" in the universe, the existence of two equally ultimate powers, one good and the other evil. Also, we must never think that sin surprised God or challenged or overcame his omnipotence or his providential control over the universe. Therefore, even though we must never say that God himself sinned or he is to be blamed for sin, yet we must also affirm that the God who "accomplishes all things according to the counsel of his will" (Eph. 1:11), the God who "does according to his will in the host of heaven and among the inhabitants of the earth; and none can stay his hand or say to him, 'What are you doing?'" (Dan. 4:35) did ordain that sin would come into the world, even though he does not delight in it and even though he ordained that it would come about through the voluntary choices of moral creatures.[3]

Even before the disobedience of Adam and Eve, sin was present in the angelic world with the fall of Satan and demons. But with respect to the human race, the first sin was that of Adam and Eve in the Garden of Eden (Gen. 3:1–19). Their eating of the fruit of

---

[3]God is "not a God who delights in wickedness" (Ps. 5:4) but one whose "soul hates him that loves violence" (Ps. 11:5), so that God certainly does not take pleasure in sin; nonetheless, for his own purposes, and in a way that still remains largely a mystery to us, God ordained that sin would come into the world.

the tree of the knowledge of good and evil is in many ways typical of sin generally. First, their sin struck at the basis for knowledge, for it gave a different answer to the question, "What is true?" Whereas God had said that Adam and Eve would die if they ate from the tree (Gen. 2:17), the serpent said, "You will not die" (Gen. 3:4). Eve decided to doubt the veracity of God's word and conduct an experiment to see whether God spoke truthfully.

Second, their sin struck at the basis for moral standards, for it gave a different answer to the question "What is right?" God had said that it was morally right for Adam and Eve not to eat from the fruit of that one tree (Gen. 2:17). But the serpent suggested that it would be right to eat of the fruit, and that in eating it Adam and Eve would become "like God" (Gen. 3:5). Eve trusted her own evaluation of what was right and what would be good for her, rather than allowing God's words to define right and wrong. She "saw that the tree was good for food, and that it was a delight to the eyes, and that the tree was to be desired to make one wise," and therefore she "took of its fruit and ate" (Gen. 3:6).

Third, their sin gave a different answer to the question, "Who am I?" The correct answer was that Adam and Eve were creatures of God, dependent on him and always to be subordinate to him as their Creator and Lord. But Eve, and then Adam, succumbed to the temptation to "be like God" (Gen. 3:5), thus attempting to put themselves in the place of God.

It is important to insist on the historical truthfulness of the narrative of the fall of Adam and Eve. Just as the account of the creation of Adam and Eve is tied in with the rest of the historical narrative in the book of Genesis, so also this account of the fall of man, which follows the history of man's creation, is presented by the author as straightforward, narrative history. Moreover, the New Testament authors look back on this account and affirm that "sin came into the world through one man" (Rom. 5:12) and insist that "the judgment following one trespass brought condemnation" (Rom. 5:16) and that "the serpent deceived Eve by his cunning" (2 Cor. 11:3; cf. 1 Tim. 2:14). The serpent was no doubt, a real, physical serpent, but one that was talking because of the empowerment of Satan speaking through it (cf. Gen. 3:15 with Rom. 16:20; also Num. 22:28–30; Rev. 12:9; 20:2).

Finally, we should note that all sin is ultimately irrational. It really did not make sense for Satan to rebel against God in the expectation of being able to exalt himself above God. Nor did it make sense for Adam and Eve to think that there could be any gain in disobeying the words of their Creator. These were foolish choices. The persistence of Satan in rebelling against God even today is still a foolish choice, as is the decision on the part of any human being to continue in a state of rebellion against God. It is not the wise man but "the fool" who "says in his heart, 'There is no God'" (Ps. 14:1). It is the "fool" in the book of Proverbs who recklessly indulges in all kinds of sins (see Prov. 10:23; 12:15; 14:7, 16; 15:5; 18:2, et al.). Though people sometimes persuade themselves that they have good reasons for sinning, when examined in the cold light of truth on the last day, it will be seen in every case that sin ultimately just does not make sense.

C. The Doctrine of Inherited Sin[4]

How does the sin of Adam affect us? Scripture teaches that we inherit sin from Adam in two ways.

1. Inherited Guilt: We Are Counted Guilty Because of Adam's Sin. Paul explains the effects of Adam's sin in the following way: "Therefore . . . sin came into the world through one man and death through sin, and so death spread to all men because all men sinned" (Rom. 5:12). The context shows that Paul is not talking about actual sins that people commit every day of their lives, for the entire paragraph (Rom. 5:12–21) is taken up with the comparison between Adam and Christ. And when Paul says, "so [Gk. *houtōs*, "thus, in this way"; that is, through Adam's sin] death spread to all men because all men sinned," he is saying that through the sin of Adam "all men sinned."[5]

This idea, that "all men sinned" means that God thought of us all as having sinned when Adam disobeyed, is further indicated by the next two verses, where Paul says:

> Sin indeed was in the world before the law was given, but sin is not counted where there is no law. Yet death reigned from Adam to Moses, even over those whose sins were not like the transgression of Adam, who was a type of the one who was to come. (Rom. 5:13–14)

Here Paul points out that from the time of Adam to the time of Moses, people did not have God's written laws. Though their sins were "not counted" (as infractions of the law), they still died. The fact that they died is very good proof that God counted people guilty on the basis of Adam's sin.

The idea that God counted us guilty because of Adam's sin is further affirmed in Romans 5:18–19:

> Then as one man's trespass led to condemnation for all men, so one man's act of righteousness leads to acquittal and life for all men. For as *by one man's disobedience many were made sinners*, so by one man's obedience many will be made righteous.

Here Paul says explicitly that through the trespass of one man "many were made [Gk. *katestathēsan*, also an aorist indicative indicating completed past action] sinners." When Adam sinned, God thought of all who would descend from Adam as sinners. Though we

---

[4] I have used the phrase "inherited sin" rather than the more common designation "original sin" because the phrase "original sin" seems so easily to be misunderstood to refer to Adam's first sin, rather than to the sin that is ours as a result of Adam's fall (traditionally the technical meaning). The phrase "inherited sin" is much more immediately understandable and less subject to misunderstanding. Some may object that, technically speaking, we do not "inherit" guilt because it is directly imputed to us by God and does not come to us through inheritance from our parents as does the tendency toward sinful actions (traditionally called "original pollution," and here termed "inherited corruption"). But the fact that our legal guilt is inherited directly from Adam and not through a line of ancestors does not make it any less inherited: the guilt is ours because it belonged to our first father, Adam, and we inherit it from him.

[5] The aorist indicative verb *hēmarton* in the historical narrative indicates a completed past action. Here Paul is saying that something happened and was completed in the past, namely, that "all men sinned." But it was not true that all men had actually committed sinful actions at the time that Paul was writing, because some had not even been born yet, and many others had died in infancy before committing any conscious acts of sin. So Paul must be meaning that when Adam sinned, God considered it true that all men sinned in Adam.

did not yet exist, God, looking into the future and knowing that we would exist, began thinking of us as those who were guilty like Adam. This is also consistent with Paul's statement that "while we were yet sinners Christ died for us" (Rom. 5:8). Of course, some of us did not even exist when Christ died. But God nevertheless regarded us as sinners in need of salvation.

The conclusion to be drawn from these verses is that all members of the human race were represented by Adam in the time of testing in the Garden of Eden. As our representative, Adam sinned, and God counted us guilty as well as Adam. (A technical term that is sometimes used in this connection is *impute,* meaning "to think of as belonging to someone, and therefore to cause it to belong to that person.") God counted Adam's guilt as belonging to us, and since God is the ultimate judge of all things in the universe, and since his thoughts are always true, Adam's guilt does in fact belong to us. God rightly imputed Adam's guilt to us.

Sometimes the doctrine of inherited sin from Adam is termed the doctrine of "original sin." As explained above,[6] I have not used this expression. If this term is used, it should be remembered that the sin spoken of does not refer to Adam's first sin, but to the guilt and tendency to sin with which we are born. It is "original" in that it comes from Adam, and it is also original in that we have it from the beginning of our existence as persons, but it is still our sin, not Adam's sin, that is meant. Parallel to the phrase "original sin" is the phrase "original guilt." This is that aspect of inherited sin from Adam that we have been discussing above, namely, the idea that we inherit the guilt from Adam.

When we first confront the idea that we have been counted guilty because of Adam's sin, our tendency is to protest because it seems unfair. We did not actually decide to sin, did we? Then how can we be counted guilty? Is it just for God to act this way?

In response, three things may be said: (1) Everyone who protests that this is unfair has also voluntarily committed many actual sins for which God also holds us guilty. These will constitute the primary basis of our judgment on the last day, for God "will render to every man *according to his works*" (Rom. 2:6), and "the wrongdoer will be paid back *for the wrong he has done*" (Col. 3:25). (2) Moreover, some have argued, "If any one of us were in Adam's place, we also would have sinned as he did, and our subsequent rebellion against God demonstrates that." I think this is probably true, but it does not seem to be a conclusive argument, for it assumes too much about what would or would not happen. Such uncertainty may not help very much to lessen someone's sense of unfairness.

(3) The most persuasive answer to the objection is to point out that if we think it is unfair for us to be represented by Adam, then we should also think it is unfair for us to be represented by Christ and to have his righteousness imputed to us by God. For the procedure that God used was just the same, and that is exactly Paul's point in Romans 5:12–21: "As by one man's disobedience many were made sinners, so by one man's obedience many will be made righteous" (Rom. 5:19). Adam, our first representative sinned—and God counted us guilty. But Christ, the representative of all who believe in him, obeyed God perfectly—and God counted us righteous. That is simply the way in which God set up the human race to work. God regards the human race as an organic whole, a unity, represented by Adam as its

---

[6]See note 4, above.

head. And God also thinks of the new race of Christians, those who are redeemed by Christ, as an organic whole, a unity represented by Christ as head of his people.

Not all evangelical theologians, however, agree that we are counted guilty because of Adam's sin. Some, especially Arminian theologians, think this to be unfair of God and do not believe that it is taught in Romans 5.[7] However, evangelicals of all persuasions do agree that we receive a sinful disposition or a tendency to sin as an inheritance from Adam, a subject we shall now consider.

2. Inherited Corruption: We Have a Sinful Nature Because of Adam's Sin. In addition to the legal guilt that God imputes to us because of Adam's sin, we also inherit a sinful nature because of Adam's sin. This inherited sinful nature is sometimes simply called "original sin" and sometimes more precisely called "original pollution." I have used instead the term "inherited corruption" because it seems to express more clearly the specific idea in view.

David says, "Behold, I was brought forth in iniquity, and in sin did my mother conceive me" (Ps. 51:5). Some have mistakenly thought that the sin of David's mother is in view here, but this is incorrect, for the entire context has nothing to do with David's mother. David is confessing his own personal sin throughout this section. He says:

> Have mercy on *me*, O God
> ... blot out *my* transgressions.
> Wash *me* thoroughly from *my* iniquity
>
> ... I know *my* transgressions.
> ... Against you ... have *I* sinned. (Ps. 51:1–4)

David is so overwhelmed with the consciousness of his own sin that as he looks back on his life he realizes that he was sinful from the beginning. As far back as he can think of himself, he realizes that he has had a sinful nature. In fact, when he was born or "brought forth" from his mother's womb, he was "*brought forth* in iniquity" (Ps. 51:5). Moreover, even before he was born, he had a sinful disposition: he affirms that at the moment of conception he had a sinful nature, for "in sin did my mother *conceive* me" (Ps. 51:5). Here is a strong statement of the inherent tendency to sin that attaches to our lives from the very beginning. A similar idea is affirmed in Psalm 58:3, "The wicked go astray from the womb, they err from their birth, speaking lies."

Therefore, our nature includes a disposition to sin so that Paul can affirm that before we were Christians "we were by nature children of wrath, like the rest of mankind" (Eph. 2:3). Anyone who has raised children can give experiential testimony to the fact that we are all born with a tendency to sin. Children do not have to be taught how to do wrong; they discover that by themselves. What we have to do as parents is to teach them how to do right, to "bring them up in the discipline and instruction of the Lord" (Eph. 6:4).

This inherited tendency to sin does not mean that human beings are all as bad as they could be. The constraints of civil law, the expectations of family and society, and the convic-

---

[7]See, for example, the thorough discussion in H. Orton Wiley, *Christian Theology,* 3 vols. (Kansas City, Mo.: Beacon Hill Press, 1941–49), 3:109–40.

tion of human conscience (Rom. 2:14–15) all provide restraining influences on the sinful tendencies in our hearts. Therefore, by God's "common grace" (that is, by his undeserved favor that is given to all human beings), people have been able to do much good in the areas of education, the development of civilization, scientific and technological progress, the development of beauty and skill in the arts, the development of just laws, and general acts of human benevolence and kindness to others. In fact, the more Christian influence there is in a society in general, the more clearly the influence of "common grace" will be seen in the lives of unbelievers as well. But in spite of the ability to do good in many senses of that word, our inherited corruption, our tendency to sin, which we received from Adam, means that as far as God is concerned we are not able to do anything that pleases him. This may be seen in two ways:

a. In Our Natures We Totally Lack Spiritual Good Before God: It is not just that some parts of us are sinful and others are pure. Rather, every part of our being is affected by sin—our intellects, our emotions and desires, our hearts (the center of our desires and decision-making processes), our goals and motives, and even our physical bodies. Paul says, "I know that nothing good dwells within me, that is, in my flesh" (Rom. 7:18), and, "to the corrupt and unbelieving nothing is pure; their very minds and consciences are corrupted" (Titus 1:15). Moreover, Jeremiah tells us that "the heart is deceitful above all things, and desperately corrupt; who can understand it?" (Jer. 17:9). In these passages Scripture is not denying that unbelievers can do good in human society *in some senses.* But it is denying that they can do any *spiritual* good or be good *in terms of a relationship with God.* Apart from the work of Christ in our lives, we are like all other unbelievers who are "darkened in their understanding, alienated from the life of God because of the ignorance that is in them, due to their hardness of heart" (Eph. 4:18).[8]

b. In Our Actions We Are Totally Unable to Do Spiritual Good Before God: This idea is related to the previous one. Not only do we as sinners lack any spiritual good in ourselves, but we also lack the ability to do anything that will in itself please God and the ability to come to God in our own strength. Paul says that "those who are in the flesh *cannot please God"* (Rom. 8:8). Moreover, in terms of bearing fruit for God's kingdom and doing what pleases him, Jesus says, "Apart from me you can do nothing" (John 15:5). In fact, unbelievers are not pleasing to God, if for no other reason, simply because their actions do not proceed from faith in God or from love to him, and "without faith it is impossible to please him" (Heb. 11:6). When Paul's readers were unbelievers, he tells them, "You were dead through the trespasses and sins in which you once walked" (Eph. 2:1–2). Unbelievers are in a state of bondage or enslavement to sin, because "every one who commits sin is a slave to sin" (John 8:34). Though from a human standpoint people might be able to do much good, Isaiah affirms that "all our righteous deeds are like a polluted garment" (Isa. 64:6; cf. Rom. 3:9–20). Unbelievers are not even able to understand the things of God correctly,

---

[8]This total lack of spiritual good and inability to do good before God has traditionally been called "total depravity," but I will not use the phrase here because it is easily subject to misunderstanding. It can give the impression that no good *in any sense* can be done by unbelievers, a meaning that is certainly not intended by that term or by this doctrine.

for the "natural man does not receive the gifts [lit. 'things'] of the Spirit of God, for they are folly to him, and he is not able to understand them because they are spiritually discerned" (1 Cor. 2:14 RSV mg.). Nor can we come to God in our own power, for Jesus says, "No one can come to me unless the Father who sent me draws him" (John 6:44).

But if we have a total inability to do any spiritual good in God's sight, then do we still have any freedom of choice? Certainly, those who are outside of Christ do still make voluntary choices—that is, they decide what they want to do, then they do it. In this sense there is still a kind of "freedom" in the choices that people make. Yet because of their inability to do good and to escape from their fundamental rebellion against God and their fundamental preference for sin, unbelievers do not have freedom in the most important sense of freedom—that is, the freedom to do right, and to do what is pleasing to God.

The application to our lives is quite evident: if God gives anyone a desire to repent and trust in Christ, he or she should not delay and should not harden his or her heart (cf. Heb. 3:7–8; 12:17). This ability to repent and desire to trust in God is not naturally ours but is given by the prompting of the Holy Spirit, and it will not last forever. "Today, when you hear his voice, do not harden your hearts" (Heb. 3:15).

D. Actual Sins in Our Lives

1. All People Are Sinful Before God. Scripture in many places testifies to the universal sinfulness of mankind. "They have all gone astray, they are all alike corrupt; there is none that does good, no, not one" (Ps. 14:3). David says, "No man living is righteous before you" (Ps. 143:2). And Solomon says, "There is no man who does not sin" (1 Kings 8:46; cf. Prov. 20:9).

In the New Testament, Paul has an extensive argument in Romans 1:18–3:20 showing that all people, both Jews and Greeks, stand guilty before God. He says, "All men, both Jews and Greeks, are under the power of sin, as it is written: 'None is righteous, no, not one'" (Rom. 3:9–10). He is certain that "all have sinned and fall short of the glory of God" (Rom. 3:23). James, the Lord's brother, admits, "We all make many mistakes" (James 3:2), and if he, as a leader and an apostle in the early church, could admit that he made many mistakes, then we also should be willing to admit that of ourselves. John, the beloved disciple, who was especially close to Jesus, said:

> If we say we have no sin, we deceive ourselves, and the truth is not in us. If we confess our sins, he is faithful and just, and will forgive our sins and cleanse us from all unrighteousness. If we say we have not sinned, we make him a liar, and his word is not in us. (1 John 1:8–10)[9]

2. Does Our Ability Limit Our Responsibility? Pelagius, a popular Christian teacher active in Rome about A.D. 383–410 and then later (until A.D. 424) in Palestine, taught that God

---

[9]Some popular explanations of this passage deny that v. 8 applies to all Christians. This position is taken in order to say that some Christians can be perfectly free from sin in this life, if they reach the state of perfect sanctification. According to this view, v. 8 ("If we say we have no sin, we deceive ourselves, and the truth is not in us") applies to Christians before they reach the stage of sinless perfection. The next sentence, talking about our confession and God's cleansing us from "all unrighteousness,"

holds man responsible only for those things that man is *able* to do. Since God warns us to do good, therefore, we must have the ability to do the good that God commands. The Pelagian position rejects the doctrine of "inherited sin" (or "original sin") and maintains that sin consists only in separate sinful acts.[10]

However, the idea that we are responsible before God only for what we are able to do is contrary to the testimony of Scripture, which affirms both that we "were *dead* through the trespasses and sins" in which we once walked (Eph. 2:1), and thus unable to do any spiritual good, and also that we are all guilty before God. Moreover, if our responsibility before God were limited by our ability, then extremely hardened sinners, who are in great bondage to sin, could be less guilty before God than mature Christians who were striving daily to obey him. And Satan himself, who is eternally able to do only evil, would have no guilt at all — surely an incorrect conclusion.

The true measure of our responsibility and guilt is not our own ability to obey God, but rather the absolute perfection of God's moral law and his own holiness (which is reflected in that law). "You, therefore, must be perfect, as your heavenly Father is perfect" (Matt. 5:48).

3. Are Infants Guilty Before They Commit Actual Sins? Some maintain that Scripture teaches an "age of accountability" before which young children are not held responsible for sin and are not counted guilty before God.[11] However, the passages noted above in Section C about "inherited sin" indicate that even before birth children have a guilty standing before God and a sinful nature that not only gives them a tendency to sin but also causes God to view them as "sinners." "Behold, I was brought forth in iniquity, and in sin did my mother conceive me" (Ps. 51:5). The passages that speak of final judgment in terms of actual sinful deeds that have been done (e.g., Rom. 2:6–11) do not say anything about the basis of judgment when there have been no individual actions of right or wrong, as with children dying in early infancy. In such cases we must accept the Scriptures that talk about ourselves as having a sinful nature from before the time of birth. Furthermore, we must realize that a child's sinful nature manifests itself very early, certainly within the first two years of a child's life, as anyone who has raised children can affirm. (David says, in another place, "The wicked go astray *from the womb,* they err *from their birth,*" Ps. 58:3.)

---

includes the process of dealing with that past sin and having it forgiven. Then the last sentence (v. 10) does include those who have obtained the state of sinless perfection — they do not any longer need to say that they have sin in the present in their lives, but simply have to admit that they had sinned in the past. For them it is true, "If we say we have not sinned, we make him a liar" (1 John 1:10).

But this explanation is not persuasive, because John writes the first sentence (v. 8) in the present tense, and it is something that is true of all Christians at all times. John does not write, "If we say while we are still immature Christians that we have no sin, we deceive ourselves." Nor does he say (as this view would hold), "If we say, before we have reached the state of sinless perfection, that we have no sin, we deceive ourselves." Rather, near the end of his life, writing a general letter to all Christians, including those who have grown in maturity in Christ for decades, John says in no uncertain terms something that he expects to be true of all Christians to whom he writes: "If we say we have no sin, we deceive ourselves, and the truth is not in us." This is a clear statement that applies to all Christians as long as they are in this life. If we say that it does not apply, "we deceive ourselves."

[10]Pelagianism was more fundamentally concerned with the question of salvation, holding that man can take the first and the most important steps toward salvation on his own, apart from God's intervening grace. Pelagianism was condemned as a heresy at the Council of Carthage on May 1, A.D. 418.

[11]This is the position of Millard Erickson, for example, in *Christian Theology* (Grand Rapids: Baker, 1985), p. 639. He uses the term "age of responsibility" rather than "age of accountability."

But then what do we say about infants who die before they are old enough to understand and believe the gospel? Can they be saved?

Here we must say that if such infants are saved, it cannot be on their own merits, or on the basis of their own righteousness or innocence, but it must be entirely on the basis of Christ's redemptive work and regeneration by the work of the Holy Spirit within them. "There is one God, and there is one mediator between God and men, the man Christ Jesus" (1 Tim. 2:5). "Unless one is born anew, he cannot see the kingdom of God" (John 3:3).

Yet it certainly is possible for God to bring regeneration (that is, new spiritual life) to an infant even before he or she is born. This was true of John the Baptist, for the angel Gabriel, before John was born, said, "He will be filled with the Holy Spirit, *even from his mother's womb*" (Luke 1:15). We might say that John the Baptist was "born again" before he was born! There is a similar example in Psalm 22:10: David says, "Since my mother bore me you have been my God." It is clear, therefore, that God is able to save infants in an unusual way, apart from their hearing and understanding the gospel, by bringing regeneration to them very early, sometimes even before birth. This regeneration is probably also followed at once by a nascent, intuitive awareness of God and trust in him at an extremely early age, but this is something we simply cannot understand.[12]

We must, however, affirm very clearly that this is not the usual way for God to save people. Salvation usually occurs when someone hears and understands the gospel and then places trust in Christ. But in unusual cases like John the Baptist, God brought salvation before this understanding. And this leads us to conclude that it certainly is possible that God would also do this where he knows the infant will die before hearing the gospel.

How many infants does God save in this way? Scripture does not tell us, so we simply cannot know. Where Scripture is silent, it is unwise for us to make definitive pronouncements. However, we should recognize that it is God's frequent pattern throughout Scripture to save the children of those who believe in him (see Gen. 7:1; cf. Heb. 11:7; Josh. 2:18; Ps. 103:17; John 4:53; Acts 2:39; 11:14[?]; 16:31; 18:8; 1 Cor. 1:16; 7:14; Titus 1:6; cf. Matt. 18:10, 14). These passages do not show that God automatically saves the children of all believers (for we all know of children of godly parents who have grown up and rejected the Lord, and Scripture also gives such examples as Esau and Absalom), but they do indicate that God's ordinary pattern, the "normal" or expected way in which he acts, is to bring the children of believers to himself. With regard to believers' children who die very young, we have no reason to think that it would be otherwise.

Particularly relevant here is the case of the first child Bathsheba bore to King David. When the infant child had died, David said, "*I shall go to him,* but he will not return to me" (2 Sam. 12:23). David, who through his life had such great confidence that he would live forever in the Lord's presence (see Ps. 23:6, and many of David's psalms), also had confidence that he would see his infant son again when he died. This can only imply that he would be with his son in the presence of the Lord forever.[13] This passage, together with the others mentioned above, should be of similar assurance to all believers who have lost

---

[12]However, we all know that infants almost from the moment of birth show an instinctive trust in their mothers and awareness of themselves as persons distinct from their mothers. Thus we should not insist that it is impossible that they would also have an intuitive awareness of God, and if God gives it, an intuitive ability to trust in God as well.

children in their infancy, that they will one day see them again in the glory of the heavenly kingdom.

Regarding the children of unbelievers who die at a very early age Scripture is silent. We simply must leave that matter in the hands of God and trust him to be both just and merciful. If they are saved, it will not be on the basis of any merit of their own or any innocence that we might presume that they have. If they are saved, it will be on the basis of Christ's redeeming work; and their regeneration, like that of John the Baptist before he was born, will be by God's mercy and grace. Salvation is always because of his mercy, not because of our merits (see Rom. 9:14–18). Scripture does not allow us to say more than that.

4. Are There Degrees of Sin? Are some sins worse than others? The question may be answered either yes or no, depending on the sense in which it is intended.

a. Legal Guilt: In terms of our legal standing before God, any one sin, even what may seem to be a very small one, makes us legally guilty before God and therefore worthy of eternal punishment. Adam and Eve learned this in the Garden of Eden, where God told them that one act of disobedience would result in the penalty of death (Gen. 2:17). And Paul affirms that "the judgment following one trespass brought condemnation" (Rom. 5:16). This one sin made Adam and Eve sinners before God, no longer able to stand in his holy presence.

This truth remains valid through the history of the human race. Paul (quoting Deut. 27:26) affirms it: "Cursed be every one who does not abide by *all things* written in the book of the law, and do them" (Gal. 3:10). And James declares:

> Whoever keeps the whole law but fails *in one point* has become guilty of all of it. For he who said, "Do not commit adultery," said also, "Do not kill." If you do not commit adultery but do kill, you have become a transgressor of the law. (James 2:10–11)[14]

Therefore, in terms of legal guilt, all sins are equally bad because they make us legally guilty before God and constitute us as sinners.

b. Results in Life and in Relationship With God: On the other hand, some sins are worse than others in that they have more harmful consequences in our lives and in the lives of others, and, in terms of our personal relationship to God as Father, they arouse his displeasure more and bring more serious disruption to our fellowship with him.

Scripture sometimes speaks of degrees of seriousness of sin. When Jesus stood before Pontius Pilate, he said, "he who delivered me to you has the *greater sin*" (John 19:11). The

---

[13]Someone might object that David is only saying that he would go to the state of death just as his son had. But this interpretation does not fit the language of the verse: David does not say, "I shall go *where he is*," but rather, "I shall go *to him*." This is the language of personal reunion, and it indicates David's expectation that he would one day see and be with his son.

[14]We may understand this principle more clearly when we realize that the various moral laws of God are simply different aspects of his perfect moral character, to which he expects us to conform. To violate any one part of it is to become unlike him. For example, if I were to steal, I would not only break the commandment against stealing (Commandment 8), but I would also dishonor God's name (Commandment 3; see Prov. 30:9), dishonor my parents and their good name (Commandment 5), covet something that does not belong to me (Commandment 10), put some material possession ahead of God himself (Commandment 1; see Eph. 5:5), and carry out an action that harms another human being and damages his

reference is apparently to Judas, who had known Jesus intimately for three years and yet willfully betrayed him to death. Though Pilate had authority over Jesus by virtue of his governmental office and was wrong to allow an innocent man to be condemned to death, the sin of Judas was far "greater," probably because of the far greater knowledge and malice connected with it.

When God showed Ezekiel visions of sins in the temple of Jerusalem, he first showed Ezekiel certain things, then said, "But you will see *still greater* abominations" (Ezek. 8:6). Next he showed Ezekiel the secret sins of some of the elders of Israel and said, "You will see *still greater* abominations which they commit" (Ezek. 8:13). Then the Lord showed Ezekiel a picture of women weeping for a Babylonian deity and said, "Have you seen this, O son of man? You will see *still greater* abominations than these" (Ezek. 8:15). Finally, he showed Ezekiel twenty-five men in the temple, with their backs to the Lord and worshiping the sun instead. Here clearly we have degrees of increasing sin and hatefulness before God.

In the Sermon of the Mount, when Jesus says, "Whoever then relaxes one of *the least of these commandments* and teaches men so, shall be called least in the kingdom of heaven" (Matt. 5:19), he implies that there are lesser and greater commandments. Similarly, though he agrees that it is appropriate to give a tithe even on the household spices that people use, he pronounces woes on the Pharisees for neglecting "*the weightier matters of the law,* justice and mercy and faith" (Matt. 23:23). In both cases Jesus distinguishes between lesser and greater commandments, thus implying that some sins are worse than other sins in terms of God's own evaluation of their importance.

In general, we may say that some sins have more harmful consequences than others if they bring more dishonor to God or if they cause more harm to ourselves, to others, or to the church. Moreover, those sins that are done willfully, repeatedly, and knowingly, with a calloused heart, are more displeasing to God than those that are done out of ignorance and are not repeated, or are done with a mixture of good and impure motives and are followed by remorse and repentance. Thus the laws that God gave to Moses in Leviticus make provisions for cases where people sin "unwittingly" (Lev. 4:2, 13, 22). Unintentional sin is still sin: "If any one sins, doing any of the things which the LORD has commanded not to be done, though he does not know it, yet he is guilty and shall bear his iniquity" (Lev. 5:17). Nonetheless, the penalties required and the degree of God's displeasure that results from the sin are less than in the case of intentional sin.

On the other hand, sins committed with "a high hand," that is, with arrogance and disdain for God's commandments, were viewed very seriously: "But the person who does anything with a high hand, whether he is native or a sojourner, reviles the LORD, and that person shall be cut off from among his people" (Num. 15:30; cf. vv. 27–29).

We can readily see how some sins have much more harmful consequences for ourselves and others and for our relationship with God. If I were to covet my neighbor's car, that would be sin before God. But if my coveting led me to actually steal the car, that would be more serious sin. If in the course of stealing the car I also fought with my neighbor and

---

or her life (Commandment 6; cf. Matt. 5:22). With a little reflection, we can see how almost any sin violates some of the principles embodied in each of the Ten Commandments. This is simply a reflection of the fact that God's laws are a unified whole and reflect the moral purity and perfection of God himself in the integrated oneness of his person.

injured him or recklessly injured someone else as I drove the car, that would be even more serious sin.

Similarly, if a new Christian, who previously had a tendency to lose his temper and get into fights, begins witnessing to his unbelieving friends and, one day, is so provoked he loses his temper and actually strikes someone, that is certainly sin in God's sight. But if a mature pastor or other prominent Christian leader were to lose his temper publicly and strike someone, that would be even more serious in God's sight, both because of the harm that would come to the reputation of the gospel and because those in leadership positions are held to a higher standard of accountability by God: "We who teach shall be judged with greater strictness" (James 3:1; cf. Luke 12:48). Our conclusion, then, is that in terms of *results* and in terms of the *degree of God's displeasure,* some sins are certainly worse than others.

However, the distinction between degrees of seriousness of sin does not imply an endorsement of the Roman Catholic teaching that sins can be put into the two categories of "venial" and "mortal."[15] In Roman Catholic teaching, a venial sin can be forgiven, but often after punishments in this life or in Purgatory (after death, but before entrance into heaven). A mortal sin is a sin that causes spiritual death and cannot be forgiven; it excludes people from the kingdom of God.

According to Scripture, however, all sins are "mortal" in that even the smallest sin makes us legally guilty before God and worthy of eternal punishment. Yet even the most serious of sins are forgiven when one comes to Christ for salvation (note the combination of a list of sins that exclude from the kingdom of God and the affirmation that the Corinthians who had committed them have been saved by Christ in 1 Cor. 6:9–11). Thus, in that sense, all sins are "venial."[16] The Roman Catholic separation of sins into the category of "mortal" and "venial," calling some sins (such as suicide) "mortal," while calling others (such as dishonesty, anger, or lust) "venial" sins can very easily lead either to carelessness with respect to some sins that greatly hinder sanctification and effectiveness in the Lord's work, or, with respect to other sins, to excessive fear, despair, and inability ever to have assurance of forgiveness. And we should realize that the same exact action (such as losing one's temper and striking someone in the example above) can be more or less serious, depending on the person and circumstances involved. It is much better simply to recognize that sins can vary in terms of their results and in terms of the degree to which they disrupt our relationship with God and incur his displeasure, and leave it at that. Then we do not go beyond the general teaching of Scripture on this subject.

---

[15] The distinction between mortal and venial sins may seem to be supported by 1 John 5:16–17: "If any one sees his brother committing *what is not a mortal sin,* he will ask, and God will give him life for those whose sin is not mortal. There is sin which is mortal; I do not say that one is to pray for that. All wrongdoing is sin, but there is sin which is not mortal." The Greek phrase here translated "mortal" is more literally "toward death" or "unto death" (Gk. *pros thanaton*). In the light of John's concern in this epistle to combat a heresy that did not confess Jesus as God who came in the flesh (see 1 John 4:2–3), it is likely that this sin "unto death" is the serious heresy of denying Christ and subsequently failing to obtain salvation through Christ. In this case, John would simply be saying that we should not pray that God would forgive the sin of rejecting Christ and teaching seriously heretical doctrine about him. But the fact that John says there is one sin that is "unto death" (rejecting Christ), does not justify establishing a whole category of sins that cannot be forgiven.

[16] On "the unpardonable sin," which is the one exception to this statement, see pp. 98–101, below.

The distinction that Scripture makes in degrees of sin does have positive value. First, it helps us to know where we should put more effort in our own attempts to grow in personal holiness. Second, it helps us to decide when we should simply overlook a minor fault in a friend or family member and when it would be appropriate to talk with an individual about some evident sin (see James 5:19–20). Third, it may help us decide when church discipline is appropriate, and it provides an answer to the objection that is sometimes raised against exercising church discipline, in which it is said that "we are all guilty of sin, so we have no business meddling in anyone else's life." Though we are all indeed guilty of sin, nonetheless, there are some sins that so evidently harm the church and relationships within the church that they must be dealt with directly. Fourth, this distinction may also help us realize that there is some basis for civil governments to have laws and penalties prohibiting certain kinds of wrongdoing (such as murder or stealing), but not other kinds of wrongdoing (such as anger, jealousy, greed, or selfish use of one's possessions). It is not inconsistent to say that some kinds of wrongdoing require civil punishment but not all kinds of wrongdoing require it.

5. What Happens When a Christian Sins?

a. Our Legal Standing Before God Is Unchanged: Though this subject could be treated later in relation to adoption or sanctification within the Christian life, it is quite appropriate to treat it at this point.

When a Christian sins, his or her legal standing before God is unchanged. He or she is still forgiven, for "there is therefore now no condemnation for those who are in Christ Jesus" (Rom. 8:1). Salvation is not based on our merits but is a free gift of God (Rom. 6:23), and Christ's death certainly paid for all our sins—past, present, and future—Christ died "for our sins" (1 Cor. 15:3), without distinction. In theological terms, we still keep our "justification."

Moreover, we are still children of God and we still retain our membership in God's family. In the same epistle in which John says, "If we say we have no sin, we deceive ourselves, and the truth is not in us" (1 John 1:8), he also reminds his readers, "Beloved, we are God's children now" (1 John 3:2). The fact that we have sin remaining in our lives does not mean that we lose our status as God's children. In theological terms, we keep our "adoption."

b. Our Fellowship With God Is Disrupted and Our Christian Life Is Damaged: When we sin, even though God does not cease to love us, he is displeased with us. (Even among human beings, it is possible to love someone and be displeased with that person at the same time, as any parent will attest, or any wife, or any husband.) Paul tells us that it is possible for Christians to "grieve the Holy Spirit of God" (Eph. 4:30); when we sin, we cause him sorrow and he is displeased with us. The author of Hebrews reminds us that "the Lord disciplines him whom he loves" (Heb. 12:6, quoting Prov. 3:11–12), and that "the Father of spirits ... disciplines us for our good, that we may share his holiness" (Heb. 12:9–10). When we disobey, God the Father is grieved, much as an earthly father is grieved with his children's disobedience, and he disciplines us. A similar theme is found in Revelation 3, where the risen Christ speaks from heaven to the church of Laodicea, saying, "Those whom I *love*, I *reprove* and *chasten;* so be zealous and repent" (Rev. 3:19). Here again love and reproof of sin are connected in the same statement. Thus, the New Testament attests to the displeasure of all three members of the Trinity when Christians sin. (See also Isa. 59:1–2; 1 John 3:21.)

The Westminster Confession of Faith wisely says, concerning Christians,

> Although they never can fall from the state of justification, yet they may, by their sins, fall under God's *fatherly displeasure,* and not have the light of His countenance restored unto them, until they humble themselves, confess their sins, beg pardon, and renew their faith and repentance. (chap. 11, sec. 5)

Hebrews 12, together with many historical examples in Scripture, shows that God's *fatherly displeasure* often leads to discipline in our Christian lives: "He disciplines us for our good, that we may share his holiness" (Heb. 12:10). Regarding the need for regular confession and repentance of sin, Jesus reminds us that we are to pray each day, "Forgive us our sins, as we also have forgiven those who sin against us" (Matt. 6:12, author's translation; cf. 1 John 1:9).

When we sin as Christians, it is not only our personal relationship with God that is disrupted. Our Christian life and fruitfulness in ministry are also damaged. Jesus warns us, "As the branch cannot bear fruit by itself, unless it abides in the vine, neither can you, unless you abide in me" (John 15:4). When we stray from fellowship with Christ because of sin in our lives, we diminish the degree to which we are abiding in Christ.

The New Testament writers frequently speak of the destructive consequences of sin in the lives of believers. In fact, many sections of the epistles are taken up with rebuking and discouraging Christians from sin that they are committing. Paul says that if Christians yield themselves to sin, they increasingly become "slaves" of sin (Rom. 6:16), whereas God wants Christians to progress upward on a path of ever-increasing righteousness in life. If our goal is to grow in increasing fullness of life until the day we die and pass into the presence of God in heaven, to sin is to do an about-face and begin to walk downhill away from the goal of likeness to God; it is to go in a direction that "leads to death" (Rom. 6:16) and eternal separation from God, the direction from which we were rescued when we became Christians.[17]

Peter says that sinful desires that remain in our hearts *"wage war* against your soul" (1 Peter 2:11)—the military language correctly translates Peter's expression and conveys the imagery that sinful desires within us are like soldiers in a battle and their target is our spiritual well-being. To give in to such sinful desires, to nurture and cherish them in our hearts, is to give food, shelter, and welcome to the enemy's troops. If we yield to the desires that "wage war" against our souls, we will inevitably feel some loss of spiritual strength, some diminution of spiritual power, some loss of effectiveness in the work of God's kingdom.

Moreover, when we sin as Christians we suffer a loss of heavenly reward. A person who has built on the work of the church not with gold, silver, and precious stones, but with "wood, hay, stubble" (1 Cor. 3:12) will have his work "burned up" on the day of judgment and "he will suffer loss, though he himself will be saved, but only as through fire" (1 Cor. 3:15). Paul realizes that "we must all appear before the judgment seat of Christ, so that each

---

[17] Paul is not saying in Romans 6:16 that true Christians will ever actually regress to a point at which they fall under eternal condemnation, but he does seem to be saying that when we yield to sin we are (in a spiritual/moral sense) traveling in that direction.

one may receive good or evil, according to what he has done in the body" (2 Cor. 5:10). Paul implies that there are degrees of reward in heaven, and that sin has negative consequences in terms of loss of heavenly reward.

c. The Danger of "Unconverted Evangelicals": While a genuine Christian who sins does not lose his or her justification or adoption before God (see above), there needs to be a clear warning that mere association with an evangelical church and outward conformity to accepted "Christian" patterns of behavior does not guarantee salvation. Particularly in societies and cultures where it is easy (or even expected) for people to profess to be Christians, there is a real possibility that some will associate with the church who are not genuinely born again. If such people then become more and more disobedient to Christ in their pattern of life, they should not be lulled into complacency by assurances that they still have justification or adoption in God's family. A consistent pattern of disobedience to Christ coupled with a lack of the elements of the fruit of the Holy Spirit such as love, joy, peace, and so forth (see Gal. 5:22–23) is a warning signal that the person is probably not a true Christian inwardly, that there probably has been no genuine heart-faith from the beginning and no regenerating work of the Holy Spirit. Jesus warns that he will say to some who have prophesied, cast out demons, and done many mighty works in his name, "I never knew you; depart from me, you evildoers" (Matt. 7:23). And John tells us that "he who says 'I know him' but disobeys his commandments is a liar, and the truth is not in him" (1 John 2:4; here John speaks of a persistent pattern of life). A long-term pattern of increasing disobedience to Christ should be taken as evidence to doubt that the person in question is really a Christian at all.

6. What Is the Unpardonable Sin? Several passages of Scripture speak about a sin that will not be forgiven. Jesus says:

> Therefore I tell you, every sin and blasphemy will be forgiven men, but the blasphemy against the Spirit will not be forgiven. And whoever says a word against the Son of man will be forgiven; but whoever speaks against the Holy Spirit will not be forgiven, either in this age or in the age to come. (Matt. 12:31–32)

A similar statement occurs in Mark 3:29–30, where Jesus says that "whoever blasphemes against the Holy Spirit never has forgiveness" (Mark 3:29; cf. Luke 12:10). Similarly, Hebrews 6 says:

> For it is impossible to restore again to repentance those who have once been enlightened, who have tasted the heavenly gift, and have become partakers of the Holy Spirit, and have tasted the goodness of the word of God and the powers of the age to come, if they then commit apostasy, since they crucify the son of God on their own account and hold him up to contempt. (Heb. 6:4–6; cf. 10:26–27; also the discussion of the sin "that leads to death" [NIV] in 1 John 5:16–17)

These passages could be talking about the same or different sins; a decision about this will have to be made from an examination of the passages in context.

Several different views of this sin have been taken.[18]

1. Some have thought that it was a sin that could only be committed while Christ was on earth. But Jesus' statement that "every sin and blasphemy will be forgiven men" (Matt. 12:31) is so general that it seems unwarranted to say it is only referring to something that could only happen during his lifetime—the texts in question do not specify such a restriction. Moreover, Hebrews 6:4–6 is speaking of apostasy that has occurred a number of years after Jesus returned to heaven.

2. Some have held that the sin is unbelief that continues until the time of death; therefore, everyone who dies in unbelief (or at least everyone who has heard of Christ and then dies in unbelief) has committed this sin. It is true, of course, that those who persist in unbelief until death will not be forgiven, but the question is whether that fact is what is being discussed in these verses. On close reading of the verses, that explanation does not seem to fit the language of the texts cited, for they do not talk of unbelief in general but specifically of someone who "speaks against the Holy Spirit" (Matt. 12:32), "blasphemes against the Holy Spirit" (Mark 3:29) or commits "apostasy" (Heb. 6:6). They have in view a specific sin—willful rejection of the work of the Holy Spirit and speaking evil about it, or willful rejection of the truth of Christ and holding Christ up to "contempt" (Heb. 6:6). Moreover, the idea that this sin is unbelief that persists until death does not fit well with the context of a rebuke to the Pharisees for what they were saying in both Matthew and Mark (see discussion of context below).

3. Some hold that this sin is serious apostasy by genuine believers, and that only those who are truly born again could commit this sin. They base their view on their understanding of the nature of the "apostasy" that is mentioned in Hebrews 6:4–6 (that it is a rejection of Christ and loss of salvation by a true Christian). But that does not seem to be the best understanding of Hebrews 4–6. Moreover, though this view could perhaps be sustained with respect to Hebrews 6, it does not explain blasphemy against the Holy Spirit in the gospel passages, in which Jesus is responding to the Pharisees' hard-hearted denial of the work of the Holy Spirit through him.

4. A fourth possibility is that this sin consists of unusually malicious, willful rejection and slander against the Holy Spirit's work attesting to Christ, and attributing that work to Satan. A closer look at the context of Jesus' statement in Matthew and Mark shows that Jesus was speaking in response to the accusation of the Pharisees that "it is only by Beelzebul, the prince of demons, that this man casts out demons" (Matt. 12:24). The Pharisees had seen Jesus' works repeatedly. He had just healed a blind and dumb demoniac so that he could see and speak (Matt. 12:22). The people were amazed and were following Jesus in large numbers, and the Pharisees themselves had repeatedly seen clear demonstrations of the amazing power of the Holy Spirit working through Jesus to bring life and health to many people. But the Pharisees, in spite of clear demonstrations of the work of the Holy Spirit in front of their eyes, willfully rejected Jesus' authority and his teaching and attributed it to the devil. Jesus then told them clearly that "no city or house divided against itself will stand; and if Satan casts out Satan, he is divided against himself; how then will

---

[18]See Louis Berkhof, *Systematic Theology* (Grand Rapids: Eerdmans, 1939, 1941), pp. 252–53, for representatives of each position.

his kingdom stand?" (Matt. 12:25–26). So it was irrational and foolish for the Pharisees to attribute Jesus' exorcisms to the power of Satan—it was a classic, willful, malicious lie.

After explaining, "If it is *by the Spirit of God* that I cast out demons, then the kingdom of God has come upon you" (Matt. 12:28), Jesus declares this warning: "He who is not with me is against me, and he who does not gather with me scatters" (Matt. 12:30). He warns that there is no neutrality, and certainly those who, like the Pharisees, oppose his message are against him. Then he immediately adds, "Therefore I tell you, every sin and blasphemy will be forgiven men, but the blasphemy against the Spirit will not be forgiven" (Matt. 12:31). The willful, malicious slander of the work of the Holy Spirit through Jesus, in which the Pharisees attributed it to Satan, would not be forgiven.

The context indicates that Jesus is speaking about a sin that is not simply unbelief or rejection of Christ, but one that includes (1) a clear knowledge of who Christ is and of the power of the Holy Spirit working through him, (2) a willful rejection of the facts about Christ that his opponents knew to be true, and (3) slanderously attributing the work of the Holy Spirit in Christ to the power of Satan. In such a case the hardness of heart would be so great that any ordinary means of bringing a sinner to repentance would already have been rejected. Persuasion of the truth will not work, for these people have already known the truth and have willfully rejected it. Demonstration of the power of the Holy Spirit to heal and bring life will not work, for they have seen it and rejected it. In this case it is not that the sin itself is so horrible that it could not be covered by Christ's redemptive work, but rather that the sinner's hardened heart puts him or her beyond the reach of God's ordinary means of bringing forgiveness through repentance and trusting Christ for salvation. The sin is unpardonable because it cuts off the sinner from repentance and saving faith through belief in the truth.

Berkhof wisely defines this sin in the following way:

> This sin consists in the conscious, malicious, and wilful rejection and slander, against evidence and conviction, of the testimony of the Holy Spirit respecting the grace of God in Christ, attributing it out of hatred and enmity to the Prince of Darkness. . . . in committing that sin man wilfully, maliciously, and intentionally attributes what is clearly recognized as the work of God to the influence and operation of Satan.[19]

Berkhof explains that the sin itself consists "not in doubting the truth, nor in a sinful denial of it but in a contradiction of it that goes contrary to the conviction of the mind, to the illumination of the conscience, and even to the verdict of the heart."[20]

The fact that the unpardonable sin involves such extreme hardness of heart and lack of repentance indicates that those who fear they have committed it, yet still have sorrow for sin in their heart and desire to seek after God, certainly do not fall in the category of those who are guilty of it. Berkhof says that "we may be reasonably sure that those who fear that they have committed it and worry about this, and desire the prayers of others for them, have not committed it."[21]

---

[19] Berkhof, *Systematic Theology*, p. 253.   [20] Ibid.

This understanding of the unpardonable sin also fits well with Hebrews 6:4–6. There the persons who "commit apostasy" have had all sorts of knowledge and conviction of the truth: they have "been enlightened" and have "tasted the heavenly gift"; they have participated in some ways in the work of the Holy Spirit and "have tasted the goodness of the word of God and the powers of the age to come," yet they then willfully turn away from Christ and "hold him up to contempt" (Heb. 6:6). They too have put themselves beyond the reach of God's ordinary means of bringing people to repentance and faith. Knowing and being convinced of the truth, they willfully reject it.

First John 5:16–17, however, seems to fall in another category. That passage does not speak of a sin that can never be forgiven, but rather about a sin that, if persisted in, will lead to death. This sin seems to involve the teaching of serious doctrinal error about Christ. In the context of asking in faith according to God's will (1 John 5:14–15) John simply tells us that he does not say that we can pray in faith for God simply to forgive that sin unless the person repents—but he certainly does not prohibit praying that the heretical teachers would turn from their heresy and repent and thereby find forgiveness. Many people who teach serious doctrinal error have still not gone so far as to commit the unpardonable sin and bring on themselves the impossibility of repentance and faith by their own hardness of heart.

E. The Punishment of Sin

Although God's punishment of sin does serve as a *deterrent* against further sinning and as a *warning* to those who observe it, this is not the primary reason why God punishes sin. The primary reason is that *God's righteousness demands it,* so that he might be glorified in the universe that he has created. He is the Lord who practices "steadfast love, justice, and righteousness in the earth; for in these things I delight, says the LORD" (Jer. 9:24).

Paul speaks of Christ Jesus "whom God put forward as a propitiation by his blood, through faith" (Rom. 3:25, author's translation). Paul then explains why God put forward Jesus as a "propitiation" (that is, a sacrifice that bears the wrath of God against sin and thereby turns God's wrath into favor): "This was *to show God's righteousness,* because in his divine forbearance he had passed over former sins" (Rom. 3:25). Paul realizes that if Christ had not come to pay the penalty for sins, God could not be shown to be righteous. Because he had passed over sins and not punished them in the past, people could rightly accuse God of unrighteousness, the assumption being that a God who does not punish sins is not a righteous God. Therefore, when God sent Christ to die and pay the penalty for our sins, he showed how he could still be righteous—he had stored up the punishment due to previous sins (those of Old Testament saints) and then, in perfect righteousness, he gave that penalty to Jesus on the cross. The propitiation of Calvary thereby clearly demonstrated that God is perfectly righteous: "it was to prove at the present time *that he himself is righteous* and that he justifies him who has faith in Jesus" (Rom. 3:26).

Therefore in the cross we have a clear demonstration of the reason God punishes sin: if he did not punish sin he would not be a righteous God, and there would be no ultimate

---

[21]Ibid., p. 254.

MAKING SENSE OF MAN AND SIN

justice in the universe. But when sin is punished, God is showing himself to be a righteous judge over all, and justice is being done in his universe.

QUESTIONS FOR PERSONAL APPLICATION

1. Has reading this chapter increased your awareness of the sin remaining in your own life? Are you able to mention any specific ways in which this was true? Did the chapter increase in you any sense of the hatefulness of sin? Why do you not feel more often a deeper sense of the hatefulness of sin? What do you think the overall effect of this chapter will be on your personal relationship with God?

2. Would it ultimately be more comforting to you to think that sin came into the world because God ordained that it would come through secondary agents, or because he could not prevent it, even though it was against his will? How would you feel about the universe and your place in it if you thought that evil had always existed and there was an ultimate "dualism" in the universe?

3. Can you name some parallels between the temptation faced by Eve and temptations that you face even now in your Christian life?

4. Do you feel a sense of unfairness that you are counted guilty because of Adam's sin (if you agree that Rom. 5:12–21 teaches this)? How can you deal with this sense of unfairness to keep it from becoming a hindrance in your relationship with God? At a level of deep conviction, do you really think that, before being a Christian, you were totally unable to do any spiritual good before God? Similarly, are you deeply convinced that this is true of all unbelievers, or do you think that this is just a doctrine that may or may not be true, or at least one that you do not find deeply convincing as you look at the lives of the unbelievers whom you know?

5. What kind of freedom of choice do the unbelievers whom you know actually have? Apart from the work of the Holy Spirit, are you convinced that they will not change their fundamental rebellion against God?

6. How can the biblical teaching of degrees of seriousness of sin help your Christian life at this point? Have you known a sense of God's "fatherly displeasure" when you have sinned? What is your response to that sense?

7. Do you think that Christians today have lost sight of the hatefulness of sin to a large extent? Have unbelievers also lost sight of this? Do you think that we as Christians have lost sight of the thoroughgoing pervasiveness of sin in unbelievers, of the truth that the greatest problem of the human race, and of all societies and civilizations, is not lack of education or lack of communication or lack of material well-being, but sin against God?

SPECIAL TERMS

age of accountability
dualism
impute
inherited corruption
inherited guilt
inherited sin
mortal sin
original guilt
original pollution
original sin
Pelagius
propitiation
sin
total depravity
total inability
unpardonable sin
venial sin

BIBLIOGRAPHY

Berkouwer, G. C. *Sin*. Trans. by Philip C. Holtrop. Grand Rapids: Eerdmans, 1971.

Bloesch, D. G. "Sin." In *EDT*, pp. 1012–16.

Carson, D. A. *How Long, O Lord? Reflections on Suffering and Evil*. Grand Rapids: Baker, 1990.

Colwell, J. E. "Anthropology." In *NDT*, pp. 28–30.

_____. "Fall." In *NDT*, pp. 249–51.

_____. "Sin." In *NDT*, pp. 641–43.

Demarest, B. A. "Fall of Man." In *EDT*, pp. 403–5.

Feinberg, J. S. *The Many Faces of Evil: Theological Systems and the Problem of Evil*. Grand Rapids: Zondervan, 1994.

_____. *Theologies and Evil*. Washington, D.C.: University Press of America, 1979.

Geisler, Norman. *The Roots of Evil*. Grand Rapids: Zondervan, 1978.

Hoekema, Anthony A. *Created in God's Image*. Grand Rapids: Eerdmans, and Exeter: Paternoster, 1986, pp. 112–86.

Hughes, Philip Edgcumbe. *The True Image: The Origin and Destiny of Man in Christ*. Grand Rapids: Eerdmans, and Leicester: Inter-Varsity Press, 1989, pp. 71–210.

Johnson, R. K. "Imputation." In *EDT*, pp. 554–55.

Lewis, C. S. *The Problem of Pain*. New York: Macmillan, 1962.

Murray, John. *The Imputation of Adam's Sin*. Grand Rapids: Eerdmans, 1959.

Peterson, Michael L. *Evil and the Christian God*. Grand Rapids: Baker, 1982.

Pink, Arthur Walkington. *Gleanings From the Scriptures: Man's Total Depravity*. Chicago: Moody, 1970.

Plantinga, Alvin. *God, Freedom and Evil*. New York: Harper and Row, 1974.

Ramm, Bernard. *Offense to Reason: The Theology of Sin*. San Francisco: Harper and Row, 1985.

Ryrie, C. C. "Depravity, Total." In *EDT*, pp. 312–13.

Thomas, R. L. "Sin, Conviction of." In *EDT*, p. 1016.

Wenham, J. W. *The Enigma of Evil*. Formerly published as *The Goodness of God*. Grand Rapids: Zondervan, 1985.

SCRIPTURE MEMORY PASSAGE

Psalm 51:1–4:

> *Have mercy on me, O God, according to your steadfast love;*
> > *according to your abundant mercy blot out my transgressions.*
> *Wash me thoroughly from my iniquity,*
> > *and cleanse me from my sin!*
> *For I know my transgressions,*
> > *and my sin is ever before me.*
> *Against you, you only, have I sinned,*
> > *and done that which is evil in your sight,*
> *so that you are justified in your sentence*
> > *and blameless in your judgment.*

HYMN

"God, Be Merciful to Me"

This is an excellent example of the words of a psalm set to music. The psalm was originally King David's heartfelt confession of great sin before God, but even today it is an excellent pattern of confession that we ourselves might speak to God.

> God, be merciful to me;
> > on thy grace I rest my plea;
> Plenteous in compassion thou,
> > blot out my transgressions now;
> Wash me, make me pure within,
> > cleanse, O cleanse me from my sin.
>
> My transgressions I confess,
> > grief and guilt my soul oppress;
> I have sinned against thy grace
> > and provoked thee to thy face;
> I confess thy judgment just,
> > speechless, I thy mercy trust.
>
> I am evil, born in sin;
> > thou desirest truth within.
> Thou alone my Savior art,
> > teach thy wisdom to my heart;
> Make me pure, thy grace bestow,
> > wash me whiter than the snow.
>
> Broken, humbled to the dust
> > by thy wrath and judgment just,

Let my contrite heart rejoice
    and in gladness hear thy voice;
From my sins O hide thy face,
    blot them out in boundless grace.

Gracious God, my heart renew,
    make my spirit right and true;
Cast me not away from thee,
    let thy Spirit dwell in me;
Thy salvation's joy impart,
    steadfast make my willing heart.

Sinners then shall learn from me
    and return, O God, to thee;
Savior, all my guilt remove,
    and my tongue shall sing thy love;
Touch my silent lips, O Lord,
    and my mouth shall praise accord.

FROM *THE PSALTER*, 1912, FROM PSALM 51:1–15

Alternate tune: "Rock of Ages"

Chapter 6

THE COVENANTS BETWEEN GOD AND MAN

What principles determine the way God relates to us?

EXPLANATION AND SCRIPTURAL BASIS

How does God relate to man? Since the creation of the world, God's relationship to man has been defined by specific requirements and promises. God tells people how he wants them to act and also makes promises about how he will act toward them in various circumstances. The Bible contains several summaries of the provisions that define the different relationships between God and man that occur in Scripture, and it often calls these summaries "covenants." With respect to covenants between God and man in Scripture, we may give the following definition: *A covenant is an unchangeable, divinely imposed legal agreement between God and man that stipulates the conditions of their relationship.*

Although this definition includes the word *agreement* in order to show that there are two parties, God and man, who must enter into the provisions of the relationship, the phrase "divinely imposed" is also included to show that man can never negotiate with God or change the terms of the covenant: he can only accept the covenant obligations or reject them. Probably for this reason the Greek translators of the Old Testament (known as the Septuagint), and, following them, the New Testament authors, did not use the ordinary Greek word for contracts or agreements in which both parties were equal (*synthēkē*), but rather chose a less common word, *diathēkē,* which emphasized that the provisions of the covenant were laid down by one of the parties only. (In fact, the word *diathēkē* was often used to refer to a "testament" or "will" that a person would leave to assign the distribution of his or her goods after death.)

This definition also notes that covenants are "unchangeable." They may be superseded or replaced by a different covenant, but they may not be changed once they are established. Although there have been many additional details specified in the covenants God has made with man throughout the history of Scripture, the essential element at the heart of all of them is the promise, "I will be their God, and they shall be my people" (Jer. 31:33; 2 Cor. 6:16, et al.).

Since the covenant relationship between God and man occurs in various forms throughout Scripture from Genesis to Revelation, a treatment of this subject might be put at several different points in the study of systematic theology. I have put it here at the end of the treatment of man as *created* (in the image of God) and man as *fallen* into sin, but it could come before a discussion of the person and work of Christ.

A. The Covenant of Works

Some have questioned whether it is appropriate to speak of a covenant of works that God had with Adam and Eve in the Garden of Eden. The actual word *covenant* is not used in the Genesis narratives. However, the essential parts of the covenant are all there—a clear definition of the parties involved, a legally binding set of provisions that stipulates the conditions of their relationship, the promise of blessings for obedience, and the condition for obtaining those blessings. Moreover, Hosea 6:7, in referring to the sins of Israel, says, "But *like Adam* they transgressed *the covenant*" (RSV mg.; so NIV, NASB).[1] This passage views Adam as existing in a covenant relationship that he then transgressed in the Garden of Eden. In addition, in Romans 5:12–21 Paul sees both Adam and Christ as heads of a people whom they represent, something that would be entirely consistent with the idea of Adam being in a covenant before the fall.

In the Garden of Eden, it seems quite clear that there was a legally binding set of provisions that defined the conditions of the relationship between God and man. The two parties are evident as God speaks to Adam and gives commands to him. The requirements of the relationship are clearly defined in the commands that God gave to Adam and Eve (Gen. 1:28–30; cf. 2:15) and in the direct command to Adam, "You may freely eat of every tree of the garden; but of the tree of the knowledge of good and evil you shall not eat, for in the day that you eat of it you shall die" (Gen. 2:16–17).

In this statement to Adam about the tree of the knowledge of good and evil there is a promise of punishment for disobedience—death, most fully understood to mean death in an extensive sense, physical, spiritual, and eternal death and separation from God.[2] In the promise of punishment for disobedience there is implicit a promise of blessing for obedience. This blessing would consist of not receiving death, and the implication is that the

---

[1] The RSV text translates, "But *at Adam* they transgressed the covenant," but the marginal note admits that this is a conjectural emendation and that the Hebrew text actually reads "like Adam" (Heb. *ke'ādām*). The Hebrew preposition *ke* means "like," not "at." The word translated "Adam" (Heb. *'ādām*) can also be translated "man," but the statement would make little sense: there is no single well-known transgression of a covenant by *man* to which it could refer. Moreover, it would do little good to compare the Israelites to what they already are (that is, men) and say that they "like man" broke the covenant. Such a sentence would almost imply that the Israelites were not men, but some other kind of creature. For these reasons, the translation "like Adam" is to be preferred. (The identical Hebrew expression is translated "like Adam" in Job 31:33 in the NASB, RSV margin, and NIV margin.)

[2] The punishment of death began to be carried out on the day that Adam and Eve sinned, but it was carried out slowly over time, as their bodies grew old and they eventually died. The promise of spiritual death was put into effect immediately, since they were cut off from fellowship with God. The death of eternal condemnation was rightfully theirs, but the hints of redemption in the text (see Gen. 3:15, 21) suggest that this penalty was ultimately overcome by the redemption that Christ purchased.

blessing would be the opposite of "death." It would involve physical life that would not end and spiritual life in terms of a relationship with God that would go on forever. The presence of the "tree of life . . . in the midst of the garden" (Gen. 2:9) also signified the promise of eternal life with God if Adam and Eve had met the conditions of a covenant relationship by obeying God completely until he decided that their time of testing was finished. After the fall, God removed Adam and Eve from the garden, partly so that they would not be able to take from the tree of life "and eat, and live for ever" (Gen. 3:22).

Another evidence that the covenant relationship with God in the garden included a promise of eternal life if Adam and Eve had perfectly obeyed is the fact that even in the New Testament Paul speaks as though perfect obedience, if it were possible, would actually lead to life. He speaks of a "commandment which promised life" (Rom. 7:10; lit., "the commandment unto life") and, in order to demonstrate that the law does not rest on faith, he quotes Leviticus 18:5 to say, about the provisions of the law, "He who does them shall live by them" (Gal. 3:12; cf. Rom. 10:5).

Other covenants in Scripture generally have an outward "sign" associated with them (such as circumcision, or baptism and the Lord's Supper). No "sign" for the covenant of works is clearly designated as such in Genesis, but if we were to name one, it would probably be the tree of life in the midst of the garden. By partaking of that tree Adam and Eve would be partaking of the promise of eternal life that God would give. The fruit itself did not have magical properties but would be a sign by which God outwardly guaranteed that the inward reality would occur.

Why is it important to speak of the relationship between God and man in the garden as a *covenant* relationship? To do so reminds us of the fact that this relationship, including the commands of obedience and promise of blessing for obedience, was not something that automatically occurred in the relationship between Creator and creature. God did not make any such covenant with the animals that he created, for example.[3] Nor did the nature of man as God created him demand that God have any fellowship with man or that God make any promises concerning his relationship with men or give man any clear directions concerning what he should do. All this was an expression of God's fatherly love for the man and woman he had created. Moreover, when we specify this relationship as a "covenant," it helps us to see the clear parallels between this and the subsequent covenant relationships that God had with his people. If all the elements of a covenant are present (clear stipulation of the parties involved, statement of the conditions of the covenant, and a promise of blessing for obedience and punishment for disobedience), then there seems no reason why we should not refer to it as a covenant, for that is indeed what it was.

Although the covenant that existed before the fall has been referred to by various terms (such as the Adamic Covenant, or the Covenant of Nature), the most helpful designation seems to be "covenant of works," since participation in the blessings of the covenant clearly depended on obedience or "works" on the part of Adam and Eve.

---

[3]However, animals were included with human beings in the covenant that God spoke to Noah, promising that he would never again destroy the earth with a flood (Gen. 9:8–17).

As in all covenants that God makes with man, there is here no negotiating over the provisions. God sovereignly imposes this covenant on Adam and Eve, and they have no opportunity to change the details—their only choice is to keep it or to break it.

Is the covenant of works still in force? In several important senses it is. First of all, Paul implies that perfect obedience to God's laws, if it were possible, would lead to life (see Rom. 7:10; 10:5; Gal. 3:12). We should also notice that the punishment for this covenant is still in effect, for "the wages of sin is death" (Rom. 6:23). This implies that the covenant of works is still in force for every human being apart from Christ, even though no sinful human being can fulfill its provisions and gain blessing by it. Finally, we should note that Christ perfectly obeyed the covenant of works for us since he committed no sin (1 Peter 2:22) but completely obeyed God on our behalf (Rom. 5:18–19).

On the other hand, in certain senses, the covenant of works does not remain in force: (1) We no longer are faced with the specific command not to eat of the tree of the knowledge of good and evil. (2) Since we all have a sinful nature (both Christians and non-Christians), we are not able to fulfill the provisions of the covenant of works on our own and receive its benefits—as this covenant applies to people directly, it only brings punishments. (3) For Christians, Christ has fulfilled the provisions of this covenant successfully once for all, and we gain the benefits of it not by actual obedience on our part but by trusting in the merits of Christ's work. In fact, for Christians today to think of themselves as obligated to try to earn God's favor by obedience would be to cut themselves off from the hope of salvation. "All who rely on works of the law are under a curse. . . . Now it is evident that no man is justified before God by the law" (Gal. 3:10–11). Christians have been freed from the covenant of works by virtue of Christ's work and their inclusion in the new covenant, the covenant of grace (see below).

B. The Covenant of Redemption

Theologians speak of another kind of covenant, a covenant that is not between God and man, but is among the members of the Trinity. This covenant they call the "covenant of redemption." It is an agreement among the Father, Son, and Holy Spirit, in which the Son agreed to become a man, be our representative, obey the demands of the covenant of works on our behalf, and pay the penalty for sin, which we deserved. Does Scripture teach its existence? Yes, for it speaks about a specific plan and purpose of God that was agreed upon by the Father, Son, and Holy Spirit in order to gain our redemption.

On the part of the Father, this "covenant of redemption" included an agreement to give to the Son a people whom he would redeem for his own possession (John 17:2, 6), to send the Son to be their representative (John 3:16; Rom. 5:18–19), to prepare a body for the Son to dwell in as a man (Col. 2:9; Heb. 10:5), to accept him as representative of his people whom he had redeemed (Heb. 9:24), and to give him all authority in heaven and on earth (Matt. 28:18), including the authority to pour out the Holy Spirit in power to apply redemption to his people (Acts 1:4; 2:33).

On the part of the Son, there was an agreement that he would come into the world as a man and live as a man under the Mosaic law (Gal. 4:4; Heb. 2:14–18), and that he would be perfectly obedient to all the commands of the Father (Heb. 10:7–9), becoming obedient unto death, even death on a cross (Phil. 2:8). The Son also agreed that he would gather for himself a people in order that none whom the Father had given him would be lost (John 17:12).

The role of the Holy Spirit in the covenant of redemption is sometimes overlooked in discussions of this subject, but certainly it was a unique and essential one. He agreed to do the will of the Father and fill and empower Christ to carry out his ministry on earth (Matt. 3:16; Luke 4:1, 14, 18; John 3:34), and to apply the benefits of Christ's redemptive work to his people after Christ returned to heaven (John 14:16–17, 26; Acts 1:8; 2:17–18, 33).

To refer to the agreement among the members of the Trinity as a "covenant," reminds us that it was something voluntarily undertaken by God, not something that he had to enter into by virtue of his nature. However, this covenant is also different from the covenants between God and man because the parties enter into it as equals, whereas in covenants with man God is the sovereign Creator who imposes the provisions of the covenant by his own decree. On the other hand, it is like the covenants God makes with man in that it has the elements (specifying the parties, conditions, and promised blessings) that make up a covenant.

C. The Covenant of Grace

1. Essential Elements. When man failed to obtain the blessing offered in the covenant of works, it was necessary for God to establish another means, one by which man could be saved. The rest of Scripture after the story of the fall in Genesis 3 is the story of God working out in history the amazing plan of redemption whereby sinful people could come into fellowship with himself. Once again, God clearly defines the provisions of a covenant that would specify the relationship between himself and those whom he would redeem. In these specifications we find some variation in detail throughout the Old and New Testaments, but the essential elements of a covenant are all there, and the nature of those essential elements remains the same throughout the Old Testament and the New Testament.

The *parties* to this covenant of grace are God and the people whom he will redeem. But in this case Christ fulfills a special role as "mediator" (Heb. 8:6; 9:15; 12:24) in which he fulfills the conditions of the covenant for us and thereby reconciles us to God. (There was no mediator between God and man in the covenant of works.)

The *condition* (or requirement) of participation in the covenant is *faith* in the work of Christ the redeemer (Rom. 1:17; 5:1, et al.). This requirement of faith in the redemptive work of the Messiah was also the condition of obtaining the blessings of the covenant in the Old Testament, as Paul clearly demonstrates through the examples of Abraham and David (Rom. 4:1–15). They, like other Old Testament believers, were saved by looking forward to the work of the Messiah who was to come and putting faith in him.

But while the condition of *beginning* the covenant of grace is always faith in Christ's work alone, the condition of *continuing* in that covenant is said to be obedience to God's commands. Though this obedience did not in the Old Testament and does not in the New Testament earn us any merit with God, nonetheless, if our faith in Christ is genuine, it will produce obedience (see James 2:17), and obedience to Christ is in the New Testament seen as necessary evidence that we are truly believers and members of the new covenant (see 1 John 2:4–6).

The *promise* of blessings in the covenant was a promise of eternal life with God. This promise was repeated frequently throughout the Old and the New Testaments. God promised that he would be their God and that they would be his people. "And I will establish my covenant between me and you and your descendants after you throughout their generations for an everlasting covenant, *to be God to you* and to your descendants after you" (Gen. 17:7). "I will be their God, and they shall be my people" (Jer. 31:33). "And they shall be my people, and I will be their God . . . I will make with them an everlasting covenant" (Jer. 32:38–40; cf. Ezek. 34:30–31; 36:28; 37:26–27). That theme is picked up in the New Testament as well: *"I will be their God, and they shall be my people"* (2 Cor. 6:16; cf. a similar theme in vv. 17–18; also 1 Peter 2:9–10). In speaking of the new covenant, the author of Hebrews quotes Jeremiah 31: "I will be their God, and they shall be my people" (Heb. 8:10). This blessing finds fulfillment in the church, which is the people of God, but it finds its greatest fulfillment in the new heaven and new earth, as John sees in his vision of the age to come: "Behold, the dwelling of God is with men. He will dwell with them, and *they shall be his people, and God himself will be with them*" (Rev. 21:3).

The *sign* of this covenant (the outward, physical symbol of inclusion in the covenant) varies between the Old Testament and the New Testament. In the Old Testament the outward sign of beginning the covenant relationship was circumcision. The sign of continuing the covenant relationship was continuing to observe all the festivals and ceremonial laws that God gave the people at various times. In the new covenant, the sign of beginning a covenant relationship is baptism, while the sign of continuing in that relationship is participation in the Lord's Supper.

The reason this covenant is called a "covenant of grace" is that it is entirely based on God's "grace" or unmerited favor toward those whom he redeems.

2. Various Forms of the Covenant. Although the essential elements of the covenant of grace remain the same throughout the history of God's people, the specific provisions of the covenant vary from time to time. At the time of Adam and Eve, there was only the bare hint of the possibility of a relationship with God found in the promise about the seed of the woman in Genesis 3:15 and in God's gracious provision of clothing for Adam and Eve (Gen. 3:21). The covenant that God made with Noah after the flood (Gen. 9:8–17) was not a covenant that promised all the blessings of eternal life or spiritual fellowship with God, but simply one in which God promised all mankind and the animal creation that the earth would no longer be destroyed by a flood. In this sense the covenant with Noah, although it certainly does depend on God's grace or unmerited favor, appears to be quite different in the parties involved (God and all mankind, not just the redeemed), the condition named (no faith or obedience is required of man), and the blessing that is promised (that the earth will not be destroyed again by flood, certainly a different promise from that of eternal life). The sign of the covenant (the rainbow) is also different in that it requires no active or voluntary participation on man's part.

But beginning with the covenant with Abraham (Gen. 15:1–21; 17:1–27), the essential elements of the covenant of grace are all there. In fact, Paul can say that "the scripture ... preached the gospel beforehand to Abraham" (Gal. 3:8). Moreover, Luke tells us that Zechariah, the father of John the Baptist, prophesied that the coming of John the Baptist to prepare the way for Christ was the beginning of God's working to fulfill the ancient covenant promises to Abraham ("to perform the mercy promised to our fathers, and *to remember his holy covenant,* the oath which he swore to our father Abraham," Luke 1:72–73). So the covenant promises to Abraham remained in force even as they found fulfillment in Christ (see Rom. 4:1–25; Gal. 3:6–18, 29; Heb. 2:16; 6:13–20).[4]

What then is the "old covenant" in contrast with the "new covenant" in Christ? *It is not the whole of the Old Testament,* because the covenants with Abraham and David are never called "old" in the New Testament. Rather, *only the covenant under Moses,* the covenant made at Mount Sinai (Ex. 19–24) is called the "old covenant" (2 Cor. 3:14; cf. Heb. 8:6, 13), to be replaced by the "new covenant" in Christ (Luke 22:20; 1 Cor. 11:25; 2 Cor. 3:6; Heb. 8:8, 13; 9:15; 12:24). The Mosaic covenant was an administration[5] of detailed written laws given for a time to restrain the sins of the people and to be a custodian to point people to Christ. Paul says, "Why then the law? It was added because of transgressions, till the offspring should come to whom the promise had been made" (Gal. 3:19), and, "The law was our custodian until Christ came" (Gal. 3:24).

We should not assume that there was no grace available to people from Moses until Christ, because the promise of salvation by faith that God had made to Abraham remained in force:

> Now the promises were made to Abraham and to his offspring ... *the law,* which came four hundred and thirty years afterward, *does not annul a covenant previously ratified by God,* so as to make the promise void. For if the inheritance is by the law, it is no longer by promise; but God gave it to Abraham by a promise. (Gal. 3:16–18)

Moreover, although the sacrificial system of the Mosaic covenant did not really take away sins (Heb. 10:1–4), it foreshadowed the bearing of sin by Christ, the perfect high priest who was also the perfect sacrifice (Heb. 9:11–28). Nevertheless, the Mosaic covenant itself, with all its detailed laws, could not save people. It is not that the laws were wrong in themselves, for they were given by a holy God, but they had no power to give people new life, and the people were not able to obey them perfectly: "Is the law then against the promises of God? Certainly not; for if a law had been given which could make alive, then righteousness would indeed be by the law" (Gal. 3:21). Paul realizes that the Holy Spirit working within us can empower us to obey God in a way that the Mosaic law never could, for he says that

---

[4]The covenant promises to Abraham were renewed and further assurances given when God spoke with David (see esp. 2 Sam. 7:5–16; cf. Jer. 33:19–22), giving to David the promise that a Davidic king would reign over the people of God forever. For an excellent discussion of the continuity of God's promises as seen in the covenants made with Abraham and David, and in the new covenant, see Thomas E. McComiskey, *The Covenants of Promise: A Theology of the Old Testament Covenants* (Grand Rapids: Baker, 1985), esp. pp. 59–93.

[5]For an excellent discussion of the difference between the overarching covenant of promise and the various "administrative covenants" that God used at different times, see McComiskey, *Covenants of Promise,* esp. pp. 139–77 and 193–211.

God "has made us competent to be ministers of a new covenant, not in a written code but in the Spirit; for the written code kills, but the Spirit gives life" (2 Cor. 3:6).

The new covenant in Christ, then, is far better because it fulfills the promises made in Jeremiah 31:31–34, as quoted in Hebrews 8:

> But as it is, Christ has obtained a ministry which is as much more excellent than the old as the covenant he mediates is better, since it is enacted on better promises. For if that first covenant had been faultless, there would have been no occasion for a second.
>
> For he finds fault with them when he says:
>
> > "The days will come, says the Lord,
> > when I will establish a new covenant with the house of Israel
> > and with the house of Judah;
> > not like the covenant that I made with their fathers
> > on the day when I took them by the hand
> > to lead them out of the land of Egypt;
> > for they did not continue in my covenant,
> > and so I paid no heed to them, says the Lord.
> > This is the covenant that I will make with the house of Israel
> > after those days, says the Lord:
> > I will put my laws into their minds,
> > and write them on their hearts,
> > and I will be their God,
> > and they shall be my people.
> > And they shall not teach every one his fellow
> > or every one his brother, saying, 'Know the Lord,'
> > for all shall know me,
> > from the least of them to the greatest.
> > For I will be merciful toward their iniquities,
> > and I will remember their sins no more."
>
> In speaking of a new covenant he treats the first as obsolete. And what is becoming obsolete and growing old is ready to vanish away. (Heb. 8:6–13)

In this new covenant, there are far greater blessings, for Jesus the Messiah has come; he has lived, died, and risen among us, atoning once for all for our sins (Heb. 9:24–28); he has revealed God most fully to us (John 1:14; Heb. 1:1–3); he has poured out the Holy Spirit on all his people in new covenant power (Acts 1:8; 1 Cor. 12:13; 2 Cor. 3:4–18); he has written his laws on our hearts (Heb. 8:10). This new covenant is the "eternal covenant" (Heb. 13:20) in Christ, through which we shall forever have fellowship with God, and he shall be our God, and we shall be his people.

QUESTIONS FOR PERSONAL APPLICATION

1. Before reading this chapter, had you thought of your relationship to God in terms of a "covenant"? Does it give you any added degree of certainty or sense of security in your relationship to God to know that he governs that relationship by a set of promises that he will never change?

2. If you were to think of the relationship between God and yourself personally in terms of a covenant, whereby you and God are the only two parties involved, then what would be the conditions of this covenant between you and God? Are you now fulfilling those conditions? What role does Christ play in the covenant relationship between you and God? What are the blessings God promises to you if you fulfill those conditions? What are the signs of participation in this covenant? Does this understanding of the covenant increase your appreciation of baptism and the Lord's Supper?

SPECIAL TERMS

covenant
covenant of grace
covenant of redemption
covenant of works
new covenant
old covenant

BIBLIOGRAPHY

Archer, G. L. "Covenant." In *EDT*, pp. 276–78.
Collins, G. N. M. "Federal Theology." In *EDT*, pp. 413–14.
Dumbrell, W. J. *Covenant and Creation*. Nashville: Thomas Nelson, 1984.
Fuller, Daniel P. *Gospel and Law: Contrast or Continuum? The Hermeneutics of Dispensationalism and Covenant Theology*. Grand Rapids: Eerdmans, 1980.
Jocz, Jakob. *The Covenant: A Theology of Human Destiny*. Grand Rapids: Eerdmans, 1968.
Kaiser, Walter C., Jr. *Toward An Old Testament Theology*. Grand Rapids: Zondervan, 1978.
Martens, Elmer. *God's Design: A Focus on Old Testament Theology*. Grand Rapids: Baker, 1981.
McComiskey, Thomas E. *The Covenants of Promise: A Theology of the Old Testament Covenants*. Grand Rapids: Baker, 1985.
Murray, John. *Covenant of Grace*. London: Tyndale, 1954.
Osterhaven, M. E. "Covenant Theology." In *EDT*, pp. 279–80.
Pentecost, J. Dwight. *Thy Kingdom Come*. Wheaton, Ill.: Scripture Press, 1990.
Peters, G. N. H. *The Theocratic Kingdom*. 3 vols. New York: Funk and Wagnalls, 1952 (first published 1884).
Rayburn, R. S. "Covenant, The New." In *EDT*, pp. 278–79.
Robertson, O. Palmer. *The Christ of the Covenants*. Grand Rapids: Baker, 1980.
Ryrie, C. C. *Dispensationalism Today*. Chicago: Moody, 1965.
VanGemeren, Willem. *The Progress of Redemption*. Grand Rapids: Zondervan, 1988.

CHAPTER 6 · THE COVENANTS BETWEEN GOD AND MAN

SCRIPTURE MEMORY PASSAGE

Hebrews 8:10:

> *"This is the covenant that I will make with the house of Israel after those days," says the Lord:*
> *"I will put my laws into their minds,*
> *and write them on their hearts,*
> *and I will be their God,*
> *and they shall be my people."*

HYMN

"Trust and Obey"

This hymn reminds us that the enjoyment of God's blessings depends on our continuing to fulfill the conditions of faith and obedience as stipulated in the New Testament, which is the written record of the provisions of the new covenant that God has made with us.

When we walk with the Lord in the light of his Word,
    What a glory he sheds on our way!
While we do his good will, he abides with us still,
    And with all who will trust and obey.

Chorus:
Trust and obey, for there's no other way
    To be happy in Jesus, but to trust and obey.

Not a shadow can rise, not a cloud in the skies,
But his smile quickly drives it away;
    Not a doubt or a fear, not a sigh nor a tear,
Can abide while we trust and obey.

Not a burden we bear, not a sorrow we share,
But our toil he doth richly repay;
    Not a grief nor a loss, not a frown or a cross,
But is blest if we trust and obey.

But we never can prove the delights of his love
Until all on the altar we lay;
    For the favor he shows, and the joy he bestows,
Are for them who will trust and obey.

Then in fellowship sweet we will sit at his feet,
Or we'll walk by his side in the way;
    What he says we will do, where he sends we will go,
Never fear, only trust and obey.

AUTHOR: JAMES H. SAMMIS, D. 1919

We want to hear from you. Please send your comments about this book to us in care of zreview@zondervan.com. Thank you.

www.ingramcontent.com/pod-product-compliance
Lightning Source LLC
Chambersburg PA
CBHW081324040426
42453CB00013B/2294